Arthur C Echternacht

How Reptiles and Amphibians Live

ELSEVIER EΦ PHAIDON

Credits
to Photographers

Artists and photographers are listed alphabetically with their agent's initials, where applicable, abbreviated as follows: (AFA) Associated Freelance Artists Ltd. (NSP) Natural Science Photos. (Res) Bruce Coleman Ltd.

Des Bartlett (Res) 43T 89T
J. Brownlie (Res) 24 115
Jane Burton (Res) 13T 16B 42 43B 53 78 82 84R 87T 105 113 132 136
P. J. K. Burton (NSP) 64
Bruce Coleman (Res) 89B
Dr M. E. Dewar 29
Elsevier Amsterdam 27 28 30L 34 39 74 76 77 79 81B 87B 96T 119B
C. Frith (NSP) 99 119T 124
M. P. Harris 127
Dr Hoogmoed Leiden 111B, 131
Eric Hosking 129

D. Hughes (Res) 13B 90
Peter Jackson (Res) 134
Russ Kinne (Res) 80 130
Geoffrey Kinns (AFA) 38 44R 57 96B
A. Leutscher (NSP) 44L 71B
London Zoo 15
John Markham 45 73T
P. Morris 58
J. Norris Wood (NSP) 41 52 60L 62 63B 67 93 102 104 117
Denys Ovendon 26 31 35 36 37 116 121
Grace Thompson (Res) 118
A van den Nieuwenhuizen (Frontispiece) 6 7 8 9 10 12 16T 17 18 19 20 21 22 23 25 47 48 49 54 59 60R 61 63T 66 68 69 70 71T 72 73B 75 83 84L 86 91 94 95 96M 97 98 100 101 103 107 109 110 111T 112 114 128 133 135
P. H. Ward (NSP) 88
D. P. Wilson 81T 108

Elsevier-Phaidon,

An imprint of Phaidon Press Ltd.
Littlegate House, St Ebbe's Street, Oxford

First published 1977
Planned and produced by
Elsevier International Projects Ltd, Oxford
© 1977 Elsevier Publishing Projects SA, Lausanne.

ISBN 0 7290 0023 0

Filmset by Keyspools Limited, Golborne, Lancashire
Printed and bound by Brepols, Turnhout, Belgium

How Reptiles and Amphibians Live

How
Animals
Live

edited by

Peter
Hutchinson

*a series
of volumes
describing
the behaviour
and ecology
of the animal
kingdom*

VOLUME 6

Contents

Of the major groups of living vertebrates, amphibians and reptiles are, on average, the least well-known. It is really not so difficult to understand why this is the case. Fishes and fish-like vertebrates have been of importance to man since it was discovered that many kinds were good to eat and that it was often a great deal of fun to catch them. Birds too have attracted the attention of hunter and cook, and they have gathered a huge following among scientists and amateur naturalists alike. Mammals, even more than birds and fishes, have become a normal part of the daily lives of peoples the world over, as companions and co-workers, as sources of subsistance and sport. And, of course, there is the more compelling reason for human interest in mammals. It is to the class Mammalia that man himself belongs. Amphibians and reptiles, on the other hand, are of economic importance in very few parts of the world. They have only recently begun to gain acceptance as pets, and many of them are, justly or not, regarded with repugnance or outright fear. There are probably more myths and legends concerning amphibians and reptiles than there are for any other vertebrate group and most of these stories portray the animals in a negative way. Of course, many amphibians and reptiles are unobtrusive, secretive animals seldom seen unless one makes an effort to seek them out, but even this trait reinforces their bad image because they are usually encountered suddenly and unexpectedly, bringing on a perfectly natural fright response in their unwitting discoverer. Among civilized cultures, the only large group of people unfailingly curious about amphibians and reptiles and their habits are children – until they are swayed by the biases of their parents. Frogs, toads and tadpoles are highly prized by many youngsters, as are turtles of most kinds, but these interests fade as children grow older and heed their parents' warnings. In the past, only a few obstinate individuals have retained an interest in amphibians and reptiles into adulthood, and most of these stubborn types became scientists of one sort or another. There has been a considerable increase in general interest in amphibians and reptiles, however, as evidenced by the numbers of people crowded around the reptile exhibits at zoos and museums, and in the number of students in colleges and universities taking courses dealing with these vertebrates. It is my purpose in this book to provide a short introduction to these fascinating animals, to lay to rest as many of the myths as possible while demonstrating that many species are so remarkable that no myths or legends are necessary to make them interesting.

It is a little awkward to attempt to discuss both amphibians and reptiles at the same time. Although there are three major groups of vertebrates which are fish-like, all share an instantly recognizable body form and all are aquatic. Birds are, of course, remarkably uniform in appearance even though considerable size diversity is evident and some have lost the ability to fly. All mammals are likewise similar and it is doubtful that anyone would mistake a mammal for anything else. In discussing amphibians and reptiles, however, we must consider

Amphibians include the well-known frogs and toads. The Natterjack *Bufo calamita* (left) is from Europe and the Horned frog *Ceratophrys dorsata* (right) is South American.

The African Clawed frog *Xenopus laevis*, a tongueless frog sometimes classified in a separate group from other frogs.

amphibians that are snake-like or even worm-like, amphibians with perfectly 'normal' legs and amphibians with hind legs greatly modified for jumping, reptiles that have legs and those which don't, species that are fully aquatic and others that live in deserts, or forests, beneath the ground, on the ground and above the ground. A few species of tropical amphibians and reptiles are even able to glide, taking to the air to escape predators. All in all, treating amphibians and reptiles together would make about as much sense as trying to discuss birds and mammals at the same time were it not for one thing: the two groups were lumped together in both the popular and scientific mind until well into the last century and they are still thought of together by many laymen. Given all of this confusion, or potential confusion, it might be best to begin by defining exactly what is meant by the two terms 'amphibian' and 'reptile'. To avoid certain complications, we will confine our definition to living amphibians and reptiles only.

Amphibians. As the name amphibian implies (Greek: *amphi* = double, *bios* = life), members of the class are typically aquatic as larvae and more or less terrestrial as adults. Unfortunately, things are not that simple. While it is true that most amphibians pass through an aquatic larval stage before metamorphosing into adults, some amphibians are fully terrestrial and their eggs hatch into miniature replicas of the parents. There is no free-living larval stage. In some salamanders, metamorphosis never occurs and the larvae become sexually mature. A number of amphibians, although undergoing metamorphosis from larval to adult form, are fully aquatic as adults and are not truly amphibious at all. In the European salamander *Salamandra atra* (family Salamandridae), fully metamorphosed young are born, not hatched from eggs previously layed by the female. Likewise, it is somewhat of a generality to characterize adult amphibians as being four-legged animals and possessing a backbone, for one major group, the caecilians, have no legs at all,

8

and leg reduction or partial absence is known among the salamanders as well. Amphibians, of course, lack feathers or hair, and most lack scales, but some caecilians do have tiny scales imbedded in the skin. Respiration is facilitated by gills, lungs and the highly vascularized skin and lining of the mouth. Larval respiration emphasizes gills, but adults may have any or all of these, and one group of salamanders, members of the family Plethodontidae, have done away with lungs altogether, relying entirely on the skin for gas exchange as adults. The amphibian heart has three chambers, two atria and one ventricle. The skull is simpler than that of fishes, there being fewer bones, and it is jointed to the top of the backbone or vertebral column by two articulations called occipital condyles, a characteristic amphibians share with mammals, but not with reptiles or birds. There are only 10 cranial nerves, rather than 12 as in birds and mammals. The teeth of living amphibians are peculiar and unique in consisting of a conical tip and cylindrical base connected by a zone of weakness (a 'hinge'). Finally, amphibians are ectothermic, that is, their body temperature is dependent upon that of the immediate environment. They cannot regulate their body temperatures internally, by metabolic means, as do birds and mammals. The term ectothermic is much preferred to 'cold-blooded' because the blood of ectotherms may in fact be relatively warm if they are found in warm surroundings. The words 'warm' and 'cold' are, after all, relative and what is cold to one may be warm to another.

Reptiles. Just as we cannot easily define what an amphibian is in a few words, we cannot adequately characterize reptiles without considering a suite of characters. Most reptiles have scales, but not all: the soft-shelled turtles (family Trionychidae) lack them. Reptiles never have feathers or hair. Many reptiles have four fully developed limbs, but many lizards and all snakes lack functional legs. The skulls of reptiles and amphibians are simpler than those of fishes, in terms of numbers of bones, but not as simple as those of birds or mammals. They articulate with the vertebral column by a single condyle. All reptiles respire via lungs, but cutaneous (skin) respiration is evident among some turtles and sea snakes. The heart is three-chambered in most reptiles, but becomes four-chambered in crocodilians. There are 12 pairs of cranial nerves. Reptiles have no larval stage and either give birth to fully-formed young or lay eggs. Unlike the eggs of amphibians and fishes, which are relatively unprotected and must be layed either in water or in a moist place on land, the eggs of reptiles are of a type called amniotic. The transition from amphibian to reptile, or, to be more precise, the transition from aquatic to

A Nile monitor *Varanus niloticus* has a scale-covered skin, like most reptiles but unlike amphibians such as the African clawed frog opposite.

9

The common Box turtle *Terrapene carolina* of the Eastern United States. It has a high-vaulted shell and is largely terrestrial.

terrestrial, would not have been possible without the evolution of the amniotic egg which freed reptiles from dependence on open bodies of water for reproduction. There is a tough shell enclosing the developing embryo. Inside the shell, and closely associated with it, is a membrane, the chorion, through which oxygen and carbon dioxide pass. A second membrane, the amnion, surrounds the embryo itself and contains the fluid that bathes the embryo during development. In amphibians, waste materials produced by the embryo diffuse directly through the gelatinous membrane surrounding the embryo, but this is not possible in the completely enclosed reptilian egg. The amniotic egg contains a third membrane, the allantois, which serves to hold metabolic waste products and also facilitates gas exchange via its highly vascularized structure. Like amphibians, living reptiles are ectothermic, and

thermoregulation must be by behavioural means rather than metabolic.

From these brief definitions, it should be apparent that in amphibians and reptiles we see two great transition groups in vertebrate evolution. With the evolution of amphibians came the first attempts by vertebrates to invade terrestrial habitats. Amphibians themselves were never able to fully exploit this novel environment because of the need for water or at least a very moist habitat in which to deposit their eggs. But amphibians paved the way for reptiles, which gained a solid foot-hold on land and which, in turn, gave rise to both birds and mammals. Although much of the rest of this book deals with the adaptations that allow amphibians and reptiles to occupy their semiaquatic or terrestrial environments, it might be well first to discuss some of the obstacles faced by these vertebrate

the mouth and trapped there as the external nares are shut. The floor of the mouth is then raised, pushing the air back into the lungs. Exhalation is a passive manoeuvre through the mouth and open nares. In other amphibians with well-developed ribs and thoracic muscles, regular changes can be effected in the pressure around the lungs. When there is little pressure around the lungs, pressure is lower in the lungs than outside the animal and air is sucked into the lungs. When pressure is increased around the lungs, air is forced out. To use either of these means of breathing efficiently, the ancestral amphibian had to lift its body off the ground. The pressures brought about by its own weight would have countered effective breathing. The evolution of tetrapod limbs then offered a two-fold advantage, one in terms of respiration, the other in terms of locomotion. Air is a much less supportive medium than water and some change in limb structure was necessary although the fins of those fishes which gave rise to amphibians already allowed an awkward form of locomotion on land or in shallow water. A first advance was the direct connection of the pelvic girdle to the vertebral column, allowing more rigid support than was otherwise possible. This connection had already been achieved among fishes for the pectoral girdle, but the connection was via the skull, a most unsatisfactory arrangement for a terrestrial organism. Any force generated in movement overland would have been transmitted to the skull. The evolution of a pectoral girdle divorced from direct contact with the skull eliminated this problem. The vertebral column of fishes is not strong enough to support the body off the ground out of water, and with the evolution of 'terrestrial' pectoral and pelvic girdles came modifications in the articulation of the vertebrae to allow flexibility of lateral movement while restricting somewhat up and down motion, thus providing a more rigid support on which to 'hang' the body. Coupled with all of this, of course, were modifications changing fins to feet.

The loss of direct contact between the pectoral girdle and the skull allowed the ancestral amphibian to have a neck and considerably greater flexibility in head movements than is found in fishes. Whereas a fish might simply move up or down in the water column to see over a barrier, a land animal that is unable to fly would find a flexible neck advantageous in allowing it to raise its head to peer over an obstacle. In order that the head, which is essentially suspended at the end of the vertebral column, be well

pioneers and the major adaptations that overcame these obstacles.

Adaptations to Life on Dry Land. Of primary importance in the evolution of amphibians was the development of an efficient means of gas exchange in air. Gills, which must be kept moist, would not suffice. Several groups of fishes living at the time that amphibians arose, possessed lungs, but lungs alone would not solve the problem faced by an animal on land. In fishes, air can be passed to the lungs in bubble form. The fish simply gulps air and dives so that the bubble rises into the lungs. Land animals had to evolve a means of actively moving air through the respiratory passage to the lungs. There were two solutions. In some amphibians which had developed broad heads, such as is evident in frogs today, air may have been pumped into the lungs. In these forms, the floor of the mouth is lowered and the external nares (nostrils) opened. Air is sucked into

supported, the braincase of amphibians is more solid than that of fishes and serves as a point of attachment for neck muscles supporting the head.

Major changes in the sense organs were necessary as amphibians moved onto land. Although primitive amphibians and many living today retain the lateral line organs of their fish ancestors for sensing vibrations in water, these organs are not sensitive enough to detect sound vibrations in air. An external eardrum, the tympanum, appeared and changes in existing bones of the jaw resulted in an ear suitable for hearing air-borne sounds. Changes in the cornea and lens of the eye, coupled with the evolution of an eyelid to help keep the surface of the eye wet, prepared the amphibian for land vision, and mucous secretions were necessary to keep the delicate olfactory structures moist and functioning. Internal nostrils or nares were already present in the ancestral fishes and these were retained and improved to allow the amphibian to draw in air in a restricted manner, without opening its mouth and exposing the delicate lining to rapid dessication. In fact, dessication was and is a major problem faced by amphibians. It is reduced somewhat by the mucous coating characteristic of most amphibians which retards water loss but allows gas exchange and water intake when the animal is in moist surroundings.

Although fishes and the more aquatic amphibians excrete nitrogenous waste materials in the form of ammonia, as do amphibian larvae, many adult amphibians conserve valuable water by excreting urea or even, in a very few species, uric acid. Ammonia is highly toxic and must be eliminated rapidly before it can accumulate, and it is excreted with large amounts of water in which it is soluble. Urea is much less toxic and less soluble in water, and uric acid is non-toxic and not at all soluble in water. Urea and uric acid are excreted in a form more solid than is ammonia, and can be tolerated in larger amounts in the body fluids, permitting less frequent elimination and less water loss when they are eliminated. Physiological studies of certain frogs and their larvae (tadpoles) show a change-over in the enzyme systems required in handling nitrogenous wastes from those enzymes involved in ammonia excretion in the larvae to those used in urea excretion in the adults at the time of metamorphosis.

Boyd's rain forest dragon lizard *Goniocephalus boydii* (top) and the Tuatara *Sphenodon punctatus*, show how limbs are developed in many reptiles to enable rapid locomotion and even climbing.

The adaptations of reptiles for a fully terrestrial existence are, for the most part, variations and improvements on the themes introduced by amphibians. One of the most important adaptations has already been mentioned: the evolution of the amniotic egg. A second of almost equal importance was the cornification of the skin, which led to a considerable reduction of cutaneous water loss and permitted the invasion of environments uninhabitable by amphibians. Cornification of the skin eliminated the possibility of cutaneous respiration and gills are useless on land, so the lungs became more sophisticated. As reptiles evolved, the heart became functionally, if not anatomically, four-chambered, cutting down on the mixing of oxygenated and unoxygenated blood and allowing a more efficient distribution of oxygen to the tissues. Water conservation was improved by the excretion primarily of uric acid. Locomotion in tetrapod forms was improved as the limbs were pulled beneath the body, thus raising it further off the ground, although the extent to which this happened is usually not so obvious as it is in mammals.

You have probably noticed by now that it has been necessary to refer to the vertebrates we are considering individually as amphibians and reptiles. There is no acceptable collective term including both groups although some have been suggested. There was, of course, no need for a collective term prior to about the mid-1800s, because up to that time both groups were lumped into the same vertebrate class. There is a word for the study of both classes: herpetology. Scientists who specialize in the study of amphibians and/or reptiles are called herpetologists. Some herpetologists are interested primarily in the classification and relationships of amphibians and reptiles, whereas others study the ecology, or physiology, or anatomy, or distribution of various groups of these animals. In fact, there are herpetologists who specialize in the topics covered in each of the chapters of this book. In subsequent chapters, we will draw on the works of an international group of herpetologists and other kinds of scientists in order to introduce you to the little-known and sometimes widely misunderstood world of amphibians and reptiles. Hopefully, you will come away with a greater appreciation and understanding of these fascinating animals.

Other modes of locomotion in reptiles. The African tree viper *Atheris squamiger* (top) has lost its limbs and uses serpentine locomotion, while the American alligator *Alligator mississipiensis* has a powerful tail for swimming.

A Guide to Amphibians and Reptiles

CLASS	SUBCLASS	ORDER	EXAMPLES
AMPHIBIA	**Labyrinthodontia***	Ichthyostegalia* Temnospondylia* Anthracosauria*	Ichthyostega*
	Lepospondyli*	Nectridea Aistopoda Microsauria	Lepospondyls*
	Lissamphibia	Proanura* Anura Urodela Apoda	Frogs Salamanders Caecilians
REPTILIA	**Anapsida**	Cotylosauria* Mesosauria* Chelonia	Cotylosaurs* Mesosaurs* Turtles
	Lepidosauria	Eosuchia* Rhynchocephalia Squamata	Eosuchians Tuatara Lizards Snakes
	Archosauria	Thecodontia* Crocodylia Saurischia* Ornithischia* Pterosauria*	Crocodiles Dinosaurs* Dinosaurs* Pterosaurs*
	Euryapsida*	Araeoscelidia* Sauropterygia* Placodontia* Ichthyosauria*	Placodonts* Ichthyosaurs*
	Synapsida	Pelycosauria* Therapsida*	Pelycosaurs* Thereapsids*

*Entirely fossil groups

Amphibians and Reptiles

There is no answer to the question 'Exactly how many kinds of amphibians and reptiles are there?' Whereas there is general agreement among specialists as to how many living orders of these animals there are, varying degrees of disagreement exist when it comes to families and genera and there has been controversy as to which family some genera should be assigned. With a couple of exceptions (crocodilians and rhynchocephalians), there are an undetermined number of species yet to be discovered or described. In this chapter, we will be content to avoid most of the controversy by limiting our discussion to the family level and above. Our purpose will be to provide a scheme of classification that the reader can refer back to in considering the many genera and species that will serve as examples throughout the remainder of this book, and to introduce something of the tremendous diversity evident within the two classes of vertebrates we are examining.

The class Amphibia includes over 2,300 living species belonging to three distinct orders: frogs (Anura or Salientia), salamanders (Caudata or

Urodela), and caecilians (Apoda or Gymnophiona). Members of each of these major groups are readily assigned to their proper order on sight if it is recognized that they are amphibians in the first place. There is, of course, no difficulty in knowing a frog for what it is; nothing but a frog looks like a frog. The difficulty arises with some salamanders, which may look like eels, and caecilians, which may look like earthworms! A close look will, however, clear up any misidentifications and the characteristics outlined below will help you avoid mistakes.

Salamanders. Salamanders are most often encountered in the northern hemisphere. Only one family, the lungless salamanders of the family Plethodontidae, enters the tropics, and then only in Central and South America. Nine families with about 320 species are recognized. As the name Caudata implies, salamanders are tailed amphibians. Most are generalized vertebrates with four legs as adults, and they come closest to resembling in body form the extinct amphibians from which the living orders evolved. A few species have very much reduced limbs (the Congo eels of the southeastern

Amphiuma, a fully aquatic salamander from North America which has reduced forelimbs and no hindlimbs.

15

The Western red-backed salamander *Plethodon vehiculum* (top) and the European spotted salamander *Salamandra salamandra* : both have the elongated bodies and short limbs typical of terrestrial salamanders.

Easily confused with the Eel, the Giant asiatic salamander *Andrias* is fully aquatic.

United States, family Amphiumidae) or have completely lost the hind legs (the sirens of southeastern and southcentral United States and northeastern Mexico). Salamanders range from fully aquatic to completely terrestrial, and some species are even arboreal, foraging over leaves above the ground at night. Most are oviparous (that is, they lay eggs), although some species of the European genus *Salamandra* (Salamandridae) retain the eggs within the oviducts and the young are born fully metamorphosed. Fully terrestrial salamanders lay their eggs in moist places where development to metamorphosis takes place completely in the egg, there being no free-living larval stage. Aquatic and semi-aquatic species lay their eggs in water and these 'hatch' into gilled larval forms. After further development as larvae, metamorphosis to the adult form occurs in most species. Adult salamanders range in size from tiny terrestrial species measuring only about $1\frac{3}{5}$ in (40 mm) in total length to the gigantic aquatic salamander *Andrias* of China and Japan which reaches a length of about 5 ft 10 in (180 cm). Salamanders are most often confused with lizards, but they lack scales which lizards are never without. Congo eels and sirens superficially resemble eels, but both retain limbs to some extent while eels obviously do not.

Frogs. Frogs are probably the most well-known amphibians because of their wide distribution, unique structure, and importance as food in many

A pair of South American poison-dart frogs, *Atelopus varius*, show the long hindlimbs associated with the jumping habit.

17

The South American tree frog *Phyllomedusa pulcherrima* is nocturnal. Treefrogs are characterized by having suction discs at the tips of the toes.

parts of the world. They are often introduced as dissection material in school biology classes. Frogs occur on every continent except Antarctica, from above the Arctic Circle to the southern limits of Africa and America, from low deserts and rain-forests to high elevations in mountain regions. They have been the best island colonists among the amphibians and are widely distributed in the Greater and Lesser Antilles, on islands of the South Pacific, in the Indonesian Archipelago and else-where. Considerable controversy remains as to how many families should be recognized, but 17 is a good estimate. There are over 2,600 living species. As adults, frogs lack a tail and have well-developed hind legs modified for jumping. Like salamanders, frogs may be fully aquatic to completely terrestrial, and many are almost completely arboreal (the 'tree frogs' belonging to several families). Although a 'voice' is present in several amphibian and reptile groups, it is best developed among frogs where it is extremely important in terms of reproduction for

many species. Only the African frog *Necto-phrynoides* and a Puerto Rican leptodactylich give birth to living young, all other species being egg layers. Direct development within the egg occurs among fully terrestrial species but the usual mode of development includes a free-swimming larval stage called a tadpole. Adults range from about $\frac{1}{2}$ in (12 mm) in body length (legs not included) to nearly 1 ft (300 mm).

Some question may arise as to the usage of the names 'frog' and 'toad'. Thus one may hear of 'tree frogs' or 'tree toads'. The name frog is used most often to indicate a smooth-skinned, rather long-legged anuran like *Rana esculenta* (the European edible frog) or *Rana pipiens* (the North American Grass frog), whereas toad is commonly applied to any of the many species of the genus *Bufo* (family Bufonidae). If there were only the families Ranidae and Bufonidae to consider, the words frog and toad might have more meaning, although there are relatively 'rough' ranids and relatively 'smooth'

The Natterjack *Bufo cal-
amita* has the warty skin
typical of toads and not
normally seen in frogs.

bufonids. As it stands, however, there are a great
many families, genera and species of anurans which
don't comfortably fit anyone's definition of frog or
toad. It is probably best to call all anurans frogs with
the exception of members of the genus *Bufo* which
may be called toads. Use of the term 'anuran' avoids
all ambiguity.

Caecilians. The third order of amphibians is by far
the least known. These are the caecilians. Circum-
tropical in distribution, caecilians are burrowing or

A typical
caecilian,
a legless
amphibian.

aquatic amphibians without legs. Dr Edward H.
Taylor, the foremost authority on caecilian classification, recognizes four families including about 160
living species. Very little is known of the habits of
these secretive amphibians. All are worm-like in
having skin folds which mimic the segments of an
earthworm, but close inspection will reveal much
reduced eyes which may be almost hidden beneath
the skin, and a posterior cloacal opening or vent.
Unlike salamanders and the vast majority of frogs,
caecilians possess a copulatory organ. And unlike
salamanders and frogs, some caecilians have scales.
Where present, these scales originate from the
dermal (inner) layer of the skin, rather than the
epidermal (outer) skin layer as in reptiles. Life
history information on most species is lacking, but
most species seem to lay eggs which give rise to
larvae and a few species are known to retain the eggs
within the oviducts until they hatch and the young
are born as miniatures of the adults. All adult
caecilians have a unique structure, the tentacle,

19

which is probably sensory in function. It emerges from the skull near the eye or nostril and may be difficult to see with the naked eye. No other vertebrates possess such an organ. Adult size may range from about 2 in (50 mm) in newly metamorphosed individuals of some species which are about $4\frac{2}{5}$ in (110 mm) long when fully grown, to almost 4 ft 3 in (130 cm) for the Colombian caecilian, *Caecilia thompsoni* (family Caeciliidae).

The class Reptilia demonstrates greater diversity in both morphology and numbers of species than does the class Amphibia. Four living orders with almost 6,000 living species are recognized: turtles and tortoises (Chelonia or Testudinata), crocodilians (Crocodylia), the Tuatara (Rhynchocephalia), and an order containing the lizards, amphisbaenians and snakes (Squamata). Turtles and crocodilians are easy to identify, as are most of the other reptiles, but some lizards are often mistaken for snakes, as are amphisbaenians, and the one living rhynchocephalian resembles a typical lizard in its external morphology.

Turtles. Turtles are as unique in form as are frogs. All of the approximately 335 living species belonging to 12 families have a shell which encloses the body and the limb girdles. In most species the two major components of the shell, the dorsal (upper) carapace and ventral (lower) plastron, are made up of bony plates covered by large scales. The skull of turtles is unique among living reptiles in having no

temporal openings (openings on the upper side of the skull) and turtles are the only survivors of the reptilian subclass Anapsida which is characterized by the absence of such openings. Two families of turtles, the Carettochelyidae of New Guinea and the soft-shelled turtles of the family Trionychidae, lack epidermal scales but retain a bony shell beneath a leathery covering. Leatherback sea turtles (family Dermochelyidae) lack both scales and a bony carapace and plastron, these having been replaced by seven dorsal and five ventral longitudinal keels containing dermal platelets. Turtles may be almost completely aquatic, semiaquatic or terrestrial, but all lay eggs on land. Two living suborders are recognized: the Cryptodira which are dominant in terms of numbers of species and which retract the head by bending the neck vertically unless the capability has been secondarily lost, and the Pleurodira which retract the head by bending the neck sideways. The latter are commonly known as 'side necked' turtles. Cryptodires are generally distributed in temperate and tropical environments around the world, whereas pleurodires are primarily tropical. Just as there is some difficulty in applying the names 'frog' and 'toad' over the whole range of anurans, there is a problem in the usage of the common names 'turtle', 'tortoise', and 'terrapin'. There seems to be no global concensus, but I will use tortoise only with reference to terrestrial chelonians of the family Testudinidae and turtle for all others. I

A Hawksbill sea-turtle *Eretmochelys imbricata* (left). Notice the streamlined body and flipper-shaped limbs.

The Matamata *Chelys fimbriata* (right), a South American side-necked turtle which uses its snorkle-snout to breath without surfacing.

The Malayan softshell turtle *Trionyx cartilagineus* has a flattened shell covered with soft skin instead of scales. This turtle rarely ventures on land, as is indicated by the fully webbed feet.

will use turtle as the collective term indicating chelonians as a group.

There is a tremendous size range evident among turtles. The smallest adult size is less than $4\frac{1}{2}$ in (12 cm) in carapace length and less than $17\frac{1}{2}$ oz (500 gm) in weight, whereas the leatherback sea turtle reaches a length of about 6 ft (1·8 m) and a weight of 1,500 lb (680 kg). Most turtles are nearer the low end of these extremes.

Crocodiles. The crocodilians are the only living representatives of the reptilian subclass Archosauria, the so-called 'ruling reptiles' which included the dinosaurs. There is considerable disagreement among specialists as to how many families the 21 living species of crocodilians should be relegated to, but the classification I have adopted recognizes three. Alligators, caimans, crocodiles and gavials (or gharials) are tropical in distribution. All of the living species are amphibious and some venture freely into salt water. Crocodilians have a generalized body form in that they are tailed tetrapods with well-developed limbs. The skull has two temporal openings on each side (diapsid) although one of these may be secondarily roofed-over with bone. The heart is nearly four-chambered, a condition fully achieved in birds and mammals, but there remains a small opening between the two ventricles. Superbly adapted for life in water, these large predators have a laterally flattened and very powerful tail, raised nostrils and eyes so that only these structures need protrude above the surface as the animal basks or swims, a secondary palate which separates the olfactory passage from the mouth, and a series of valves which can close off the ear openings and nasal passage when the crocodilian is under water. Crocodilians are egg-layers and either build large mound-nests or dig tunnel nests. Parental care is demonstrated by some species. The reputation of crocodilians as man-eaters is well-established but over-emphasized. It is true that many species have ill dispositions and will attack humans and documented instances of this are given wide coverage by the press, but man is more an enemy of crocodilians than the reverse. All species are endangered, largely because of human activity. Hides are valued highly in fashion centres of the world and large crocodilians are becoming a thing of the past. Of course, not all crocodilians are giants. The Congo dwarf crocodile *Osteolaemus osborni* of west Africa reaches a length of only about 3 ft 6 in (1·1 m). The saltwater crocodile *Crocodylus porosus*, and the Indian gavial *Gavialis gangeticus*, both of southeast Asia, probably reach maximum lengths of about 21 ft (6·5 m).

The Tuatara. There is just one living species of Rhychocephalian, the Tuatara, *Sphenodon punctatus*. Once found on New Zealand, this reptile is now restricted to several small islands off New Zealand where it is rigidly protected. The Tuatara externally resembles a lizard and was considered as such until 1867 when Albert Günther of the British Museum reported its true identity. Members of the family (Sphenodontidae) were once distributed over parts of North America, Europe, Asia and Africa. The Tuatara head has a beak-like upper jaw and the skull, like that of crocodilians, is diapsid. There is a well-developed parietal eye on top of the head. This structure, while not so well developed as the lateral eyes, is sensitive to light and comes complete with a lens and retina. The same structure, but even less well developed, is evident in many species of lizards. Tuataras inhabit burrows during the day and forage for insects and other food at night. They are active at extremely low body temperatures for a reptile, in the 50–52°F (10–11°C) range. These reptiles lay eggs which may take up to 13 months to hatch, a very long time for any vertebrate egg layer. Maximum length is about 2 ft 7 in (80 cm), but most are considerably smaller.

The final order of living reptiles is the Squamata. The order contains three quite distinct suborders: lizards (Sauria or Lacertilia), amphisbaenians (Amphisbaenia), and snakes (Serpentes or Ophidia). Some herpetologists would consider each of these an order in its own right. Because they are so distinct on technical grounds, and because they are generally distinguished in the popular literature, I will consider them separately here.

Lizards. There are about 3,000 living species of lizards. They surpass all other reptiles in terms of number of species, and in diversity of size and morphology. They are widely distributed over temperate and tropical parts of the world, although they reach their greatest numbers in the tropics. Eighteen families are recognized here, but some of these are 'lumped' by other workers. Some lizards lack external evidence of limb girdles, but lizards can generally be distinguished from snakes by their possession of all or some of the following characters: legs, external ear openings, and movable eyelids. Other distinguishing characteristics, not apparent without dissection, include, in lizards, the presence of a pectoral girdle, distinctive modification of the diapsid skull, and a distinctive type (tropitrabic) of braincase. Lizards are primarily terrestrial and many are arboreal or partially so.

Gavialis gangeticus, a southeast Asian crocodile whose long, tooth-filled snout identifies it as a fish-eater.

The Tuatara, *Sphenodon punctatus*, the only surviving member of the once important group of fossils called rhynchocephalians.

Some even possess adaptations for gliding, but none truly fly. A few species are semiaquatic and one, the Marine iguana of the Galapagos Islands *Amblyrhynchus cristatus* (family Iguanidae) feeds on algae in the ocean. Most lizards lay eggs, but an appreciable number give birth to living young. The smallest lizards, geckos of the genus *Sphaerodactylus* (family Gekkonidae) in the Antilles, may measure less than 2 in (5 cm) in total length, whereas the Komodo dragon, *Varanus komodoensis* (family Varanidae) reaches 9 ft (3 m)! Because of their diversity of form, distribution, local abundance and the relative ease with which many species can be maintained in captivity, lizards are playing a major role in scientific studies of evolution, biogeography, population biology and ecology.

Amphisbaenids. Until very recently, amphisbaenians were classified with the lizards and, in the more distant past, they were considered to be snakes. The recent studies of Dr Carl Gans have, however, indicated that they are distinct from both. Dr Gans recognizes three families of amphisbaenians (there is no 'simple' common name as yet) and about 130 species. Their distribution is subtropical and tropical and excludes Australia and most of Asia, but includes several islands. Amphisbaenians are distinct in having an enlarged medial tooth on the premaxillary bone, in having the right lung reduced in size (in snakes and snake-like lizards, the left lung may be reduced), and a unique middle ear structure. All are burrowers and they show a wide range of adaptations for life underground. With the exception of the Mexican genus *Bipes* (family Bipedidae), which has fore limbs, amphisbaenians are limbless. No external ears are visible and the eyes are very much reduced. The smallest amphisbaenians are only about 3 in (7·5 cm) long, and the largest $23\frac{1}{2}$–$27\frac{1}{2}$ in (60–70 cm) in length.

Snakes. The classification of snakes has undergone many changes over the past few years. This has been reflected primarily in the number of families identified by various investigators. The classification we are using recognizes 11 families with about 2,500 living species. Snakes are highly specialized. All lack functional limbs although a rudimentary pelvic girdle is present in some. Snakes never have a pectoral girdle. There is no external ear and hearing is accomplished by the transmission of vibrations through the bones. The bones of the jaws are usually loosely attached to the skull and the resulting flexibility allows many snakes to swallow relatively enormous prey. Snakes do not have movable eyelids. The skull is diapsid but modified through loss of bone in the upper temporal region, and the braincase is distinct (platytrabic) from that of lizards. Many species of snakes are secretive and rarely seen by man. The bad reputation 'enjoyed' by snakes derives from a relatively few poisonous or otherwise feared types such as the large constrictors. Having adopted a limbless, 'serpentine' body form, there is considerably less morphological diversity among snakes than among lizards. Diversity is there, however, in the feeding and locomotor adaptations of these animals. Snakes also have a full range of reproductive modes from egg laying to live birth. They are widely distributed except at high, cold latitudes, although a few species in both

hemispheres are found near the Arctic Circle. They are found from deserts to tropical rainforests; under the ground, on the ground and above the ground in arboreal situations. Many are aquatic and a few fully marine, without the need to return to land even to reproduce. The smallest snakes are about 4 in (10 cm) in length, and both the Reticulate python *Python reticulatus* of southeast Asia and the Anaconda *Eunectes murinus* of South America (both family Boidae) may reach 29 ft (9 m). Greater lengths have been reported for both, but without documentation.

This brief introduction to the major groups of amphibians and reptiles has dealt only with the living. These represent the end-points of millions of years of evolution during which, at different times, amphibians and reptiles represented the leading edge in an advance that led to birds and mammals. What were the steps that led to the evolution of the first amphibians? What were the pressures that caused amphibians to forsake the water and become reptiles? Because they are no longer at the forefront of evolution as the layman usually views it, should we consider amphibians and reptiles as somehow less successful than birds and mammals? We will take a look at these questions in the next chapter.

The Four-lined snake *Elaphe quatuorlineata* of Europe is not poisonous or aggressive, but can inflict a painful bite if provoked.

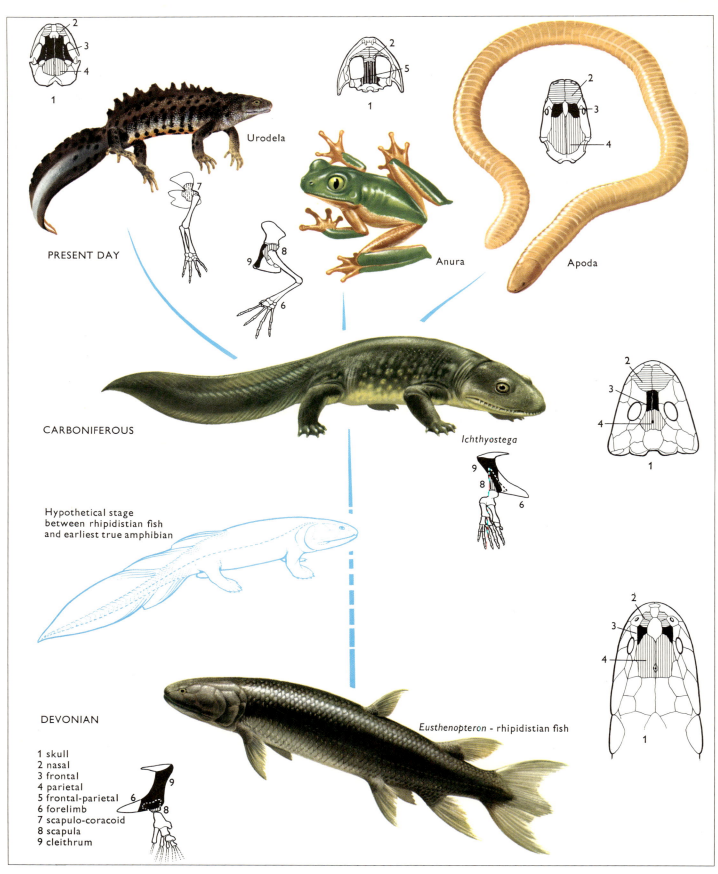

Urodela

PRESENT DAY

Anura

Apoda

CARBONIFEROUS

Ichthyostega

Hypothetical stage
between rhipidistian fish
and earliest true amphibian

DEVONIAN

Eusthenopteron - rhipidistian fish

1 skull
2 nasal
3 frontal
4 parietal
5 frontal-parietal
6 forelimb
7 scapulo-coracoid
8 scapula
9 cleithrum

26

We are here concerned with two great transitions, and these may be viewed in two ways: the transition from fishes to amphibians and that from amphibians to reptiles; and the transition from a purely aquatic organism to a completely terrestrial one. The first amphibians appear in the fossil record about 370 million years ago, the first reptiles about 300 million years ago. We are entirely dependent on the fossil record for documentation of these important steps, but that record is far from complete. At many critical points, there is no record at all! At these points we can only guess or, if the point is in the not too distant past, we may gain some more or less hazy insight into what occurred by making comparisons of representative modern forms. We will rely on a variety of kinds of evidence in this chapter as we try to reconstruct events of the past.

The Origin of Amphibians. The geological time period during which amphibians made their appearance was the Devonian. Three groups of bony fishes lived during the Devonian and might have given rise to amphibians. Two of these are the lobe-finned fishes belonging to the suborders Rhipidistia

Geological time scale.				
Era	Period	Epoch and duration in millions of years		Millions of years before today
Cenozoic	Quaternary	Pleistocene	1	1
	Tertiary	Pliocene	10	11
		Miocene	14	25
		Oligocene	15	40
		Eocene	20	60
		Paleocene	10	70 ± 2
Mesozoic	Cretaceous		65	135 ± 5
	Jurassic		45	180 ± 5
	Triassic		45	225 ± 5
Paleozoic	Permian		45	270 ± 5
	Carboniferous	Pennsylvanian	80	
		Mississippian		350 ± 10
	Devonian		50	400 ± 10
	Silurian		40	440 ± 10
	Ordovician		60	500 ± 15
	Cambrian		100	600 ± 20
Precambrian			3000 +	

and Coelacanthini of the order Crossopterygii. The Rhipidistia are entirely extinct and the coelacanths are represented only by the now famous *Latimeria*. The third group consists of the crossopterygian order Dipnoi, the lungfishes, which has three living genera, one each in Africa, South America and Australia. For a while, the dipnoans were leading candidates for the immediate ancestor of the first amphibian. The living lungfishes endure drying of their habitats in cocoons in the mud. They have both gills and lungs and rely on the latter in periods of drought. Dipnoans were, however, eliminated from consideration because their very weak paired fins could not possibly have given rise to the tetrapod limbs of amphibians, and because of the difficulty in deriving an amphibian skull from that of primitive dipnoans. Coelacanths are and were equipped with a bony skeleton in the lobes of the fins and have the musculature necessary to move these, but other anatomical considerations remove these too from contention. The evidence all points to the rhipidistian crossopterygians as the group from which

The evolution of amphibians (far left) has produced three living groups which differ in their skull bone patterns and pectoral girdles.

The skull of a labyrinthodont, the fossil amphibian *Palaeogyrinus*, with a cross-section of its tooth to show the characteristic folds.

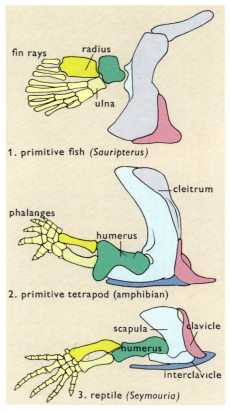

1. primitive fish (*Sauripterus*)

2. primitive tetrapod (amphibian)

3. reptile (*Seymouria*)

The evolution of the pentadactyl (5-fingered) limb from the paired fins of early fishes (1), to amphibians (2) and reptiles (3), involved changes in the shape of the shoulder girdle (scapula, clavicle and interclavicle).

amphibians evolved. The skull of *Eusthenopteron*, a rhipidistian, is similar in many respects to that of *Ichthyostega*, one of the best studied early amphibians. By way of example, rhipidistian fishes had a transverse hinge across the skull which allowed some movement of the front and back parts of the skull relative to one another. This hinge seems to be unique among vertebrates, but traces of it are found in the skull of *Ichthyostega*. Also, rhipidistians and early amphibians both possessed labyrinthodont dentition. That is, the internal structure of the teeth, when viewed in cross-section, consisted of many complex folds. Although it may be conceded that rhipidistian crossopterygians gave rise to amphibians, the record does not allow us to be specific as to exactly which of the rhipidistian families was or were involved. This is no small point because on it hinges the various hypotheses concerning the origins and relationships of the living orders.

Relationships Between Modern Amphibian Groups. The five alternative hypotheses concerning the origins and relationships of the modern orders of amphibians have been summarized by Thomas S. Parsons of the University of Toronto and Ernest E. Williams of Harvard University. Four of the hypotheses call for a polyphyletic origin. In other words, they suggest that the living orders arose independently from different rhipidistian families or that two of the modern orders evolved from one family while the other arose from a second. The second hypothesis either suggests that salamanders and caecilians had a common ancestor whereas frogs arose from a different group, or that the salamanders and frogs had a common origin with caecilians having a separate, independent origin. These three hypotheses have received varying degrees of support from students of amphibian evolution; a fourth possible hypothesis, that proposing a common ancestor for frogs and caecilians and a separate origin for salamanders, has never been taken seriously because the differences between frogs and caecilians are so great.

The fifth hypothesis is a monophyletic one, arguing for a close relationship among the living orders, and this is championed by Parsons and Williams. They call attention to a series of characters held in common by the living orders and which appear nowhere else among vertebrates, and to other characteristics which are shared by frogs, salamanders and caecilians but which are also found in some other vertebrate groups. Seven characters are considered of prime importance. All living amphibians, as well as all extinct members of modern orders for which a fossil record exists, have hinged or pedicellate teeth. Whereas hinged teeth are known to occur in some bony fishes, the hinge is not in the same position as it is in amphibians. All modern orders have fat bodies associated with the gonads. Again, fat bodies are known in other groups. Reptiles have them, but they are not very closely associated with the reproductive structures. Both frogs and salamanders have a unique set of middle ear bones, the so-called operculum-plectrum complex. In the inner ear, the three living orders share a distinct sensory area, the papilla amphibiorum. Both frogs and salamanders have, in the eyes, special visual cells, the green rods, that are lacking in other vertebrates. They are absent as well in caecilians but that might be expected, given the degenerate nature of the eyes in these burrowing amphibians. Finally, all amphibians belonging to the modern orders have similar and unique skin glands, and all have a well-developed system for cutaneous respiration (gas exchange through the skin). Parsons and Williams believe that the weight of evidence is in favour of a monophyletic origin of frogs, salamanders and caecilians and have proposed that they be united under a subclass Lissamphibia in the class Amphibia. This suggestion has met with some approval but that there is still controversy is reflected in the classifications presented in most reference books. Although strongly advocating the adoption of the subclass Lissamphibia, Parsons and Williams have not been able to identify the common ancestor required. But then, advocates of other hypotheses have not conclusively identified ancestral groups either and resolution of the problem awaits the discovery, if it is to be forthcoming, of additional evidence from the fossil record. You might have noticed, however, that most of the characters deemed most important by Parsons and Williams would not, in any case, be preserved in that record.

Early Amphibian History. Just as there have been multiple hypotheses relating to the origin of amphibians and to the origin of the modern orders, so has there been controversy concerning the question of why amphibians evolved. One suggestion has been that the ancestral crossopterygians left the water to find water! The Devonian was, at times, a period of drought and there would have been a distinct advantage for any aquatic organism that could leave a pool that was drying up in search of another which still contained water. This might have been done at night, when temperatures were lower and humidity higher. Movement might not have been too difficult for these lobe-finned fishes, and they already had the lungs necessary for aerial

respiration. It might also have been that the first amphibians left the water occasionally to escape predators. As crossopterygians were fairly impressive predators themselves, it seems likely that smaller lobe-fins might have had to escape from larger ones and a good way to do so would have been to simply leave the water or at least to enter water so shallow that larger individuals could not follow. If they began to spend more time on land, possibly at night, they might have begun to exploit a new source of food: the abundance of terrestrial arthropods. Such new opportunities are the substance of evolution, but we can only speculate. We will probably never know the answer to this question.

Having arrived on land, at least partially, amphibians underwent a dramatic radiation as evidenced in the classification presented in the preceding chapter. The Ichthyostegalia were in many ways intermediate between crossopterygians and amphibians. The hind part of the skull was long relative to that of the later amphibians but shorter than that of fishes when compared to the anterior part of the skull (the snout). The lateral line system, a sensory system found in fishes, was present and this suggests that ichthyostegans were still highly aquatic. The tail fin was supported by fin rays, another legacy of the fishes. The known families are represented by fossils from North America, Greenland and Europe. The temnospondyles were widespread and abundant from the Devonian until the

Frogs first made an appearance about 200 million years ago, and were not very different from modern forms, such as this Running frog.

The evolution of the Reptilia (right). Since their origins about 350 million years ago many more groups evolved and became extinct than survive today.

Upper (1) and side (2) views of an anapsid skull, showing the solid skull roof without perforation behind the eye socket (in other words, without temporal openings). This type of skull is found in the most primitive reptiles.

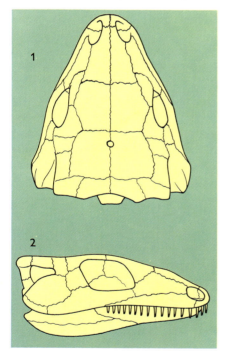

PRESENT DAY

turtles   snakes   li

CENOZOIC

Anapsida

CRETACEOUS

Archelon

rhyncocephi

JURASSIC

to mammals

TRIASSIC

therapsids

procolophonids   pareiasaurs

Cynognathus   *Dimetrodo*

PERMIAN

Pareiasaurus

CARBONIFEROUS

pelyco

OVENDEN

Triassic. They were represented by aquatic, freshwater forms, terrestrial species and, possibly, even marine forms. There are probably more genera of rhachitomes known than any other extinct group of amphibian and some, such as *Eryops*, were quite large. *Eryops* reached a length of about 5 ft (1·5 m). The other two temnospondylous suborders were remarkable yet unsuccessful evolutionary experiments. The Stereospondyli were secondarily aqua-

tic. That is, they were most likely derived from more terrestrial amphibian ancestors. They were probably bottom-dwellers and the limbs were very much reduced in size. One genus. *Mastodonsaurus*, a European amphibian, has a skull length of almost a yard! The Plagiosauria, on the other hand, had a short, broad skull. They were also well equipped with dorsal and ventral armour and the best known genus, *Gerrothorax*, retained gills as an adult in-

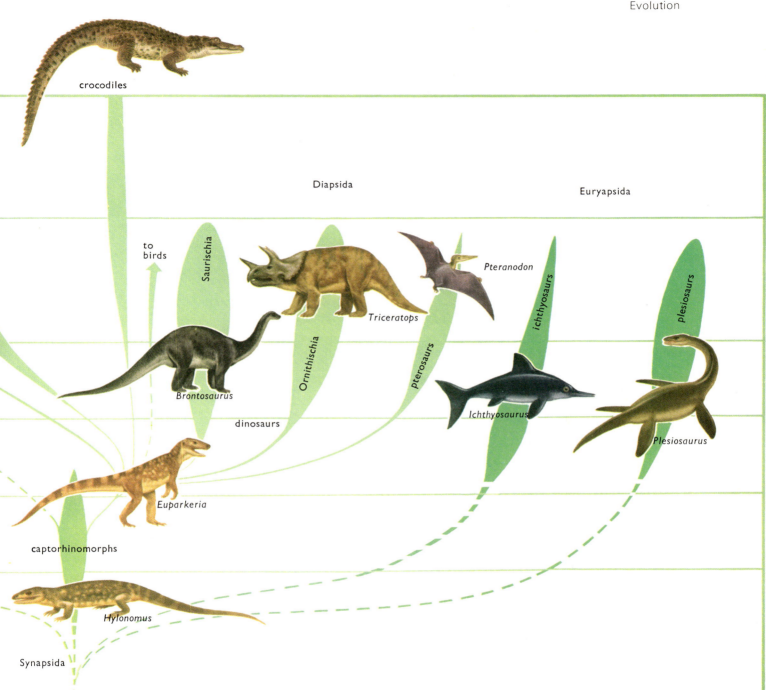

crocodiles

Diapsida

Euryapsida

to birds

Saurischia

Triceratops

Pteranodon

ichthyosaurs

plesiosaurs

Ornithischia

Brontosaurus

Pterosaurs

Ichthyosaurus

Plesiosaurus

dinosaurs

Euparkeria

captorhinomorphs

Hylonomus

Synapsida

dicating that it was neotenic. Neoteny is the retention of larval characteristics in the adults and, as we will see later, occurs in several modern salamanders. The final labyrinthodont order, the Anthracosauria, lived only from the Lower Carboniferous (Mississippian) until the Permian and they are not well known. They are, however, of interest because they gave rise to the reptiles. Both terrestrial and aquatic forms are known and the dentition of

the embolomeres suggests that they were fish-eaters. The seymouriamorphs were intermediate between amphibians and reptiles although probably not on a direct line between the two classes. Most were heavy-bodied forms that may have been highly terrestrial although the gilled larval stage of one genus has been found. There is no well-defined gap separating these amphibians and reptiles and some, especially the seymouriamorphs belonging to the family Diadectidae, have been considered amphibians by certain paleontologists, reptiles by others. Among the orders of the subclass Lepospondyli, the Aistopoda were the most unusual. These amphibians were snake-like in having no limbs or limb girdles and a large number (up to 200) of vertebrae. Although highly specialized, they are among the oldest of amphibians because limbless aistopods are known from the Lower Carboniferous, indicating that their ancestors must have been around in the Devonian. They, like the other lepospondyls, were aquatic. In some classifications, the salamanders and caecilians are included in the Lepospondyli to the exclusion of the frogs.

The Origin of Reptiles. I have already mentioned that there is no sharp dividing line between amphibians and reptiles in the fossil record even though the two classes are easily distinguished today. The early history of the amphibian-reptile transition has been studied most thoroughly by Robert L. Carroll of McGill University in Montreal. He has investigated the unusual deposits at two localities in Nova Scotia that contain the upright remains of hollow lycopsid stumps. Lycopsids are a primitive group of plants and their giant stumps apparently acted as traps for a great many amphibians and at least three genera of primitive reptiles: *Paleothyris* and *Hylonomus* are members of the anapsid order Cotylosauria, and *Protoclepsydrops* is a synapsid of the order Pelycosauria. This fortuitous assemblage is representative of the ancestors of all other reptilian groups and, because the deposits are Lower Upper Carboniferous (Lower Pennsylvanian) in age, is indicative of a very early, major dichotomy in reptilian history. *Hylonomus* seems very close to a line leading to squamates, crocodilians, turtles and many extinct groups, and *Protoclepsydrops* is a member of the group which gave rise to the mammals. *Hylonomus* was quite lizard-like although it had a skull with no temporal openings, and Carroll believes it and *Protoclepsydrops* to be similar enough to have had a common ancestor sometime in the middle Carboniferous. Captorhinomorphs are considered the most primitive reptiles, having evolved from an unknown anthracosaurian ancestor. Most investigators believe reptiles had a monophyletic origin, but there is some disagreement as to whether or not anthracosaurs were the ancestral group: other paleontologists favour a polyphyletic origin for the class.

As we have seen, the achievement of an amniotic egg allowed the final escape by vertebrates from life in the water, and this led to the evolution of reptiles. There has been considerable debate about why such an egg evolved, and whether the egg or the adult reptiles became terrestrial first. It has been argued that the amphibian ancestors of reptiles were highly terrestrial, much as certain of the living salamanders, and that the development of the amniotic egg followed naturally. Carroll's studies in Nova Scotia support this view in that the early reptiles there were obviously fully terrestrial. Alfred S. Romer, of Harvard University, has taken a different view. He and others have suggested that the earliest reptiles were semi-aquatic and came ashore to lay their eggs just as turtles and many sea snakes do today. Romer believed that the advantage of this arrangement was related to frequent drought conditions which might have threatened with dessication eggs placed in shallow water. Joseph A. Tihen, on the other hand, thinks it more likely that the impetus was avoidance of predators that might have attacked eggs or larvae in the water. Most of the potential egg predators of the time were aquatic and obvious advantages would accrue if eggs were layed on land. Tihen also argues that the transition from an unprotected amphibian egg to an amniotic egg with a relatively dessication-resistant shell would have been gradual and would have required humid conditions on land, conditions not likely to be found in times of drought.

By the end of the Triassic, the amphibian 'explosion' was over and only the lissamphibians remained. But if the amphibian radiation during the Carboniferous and Permian periods was dramatic, the Mesozoic radiation of the reptiles was spectacular! Reptiles very quickly occupied all of those ecological roles (niches) that mammals largely occupy today, and one group of archosaurs, the famous pterosaurs, were air-borne. Primitive cotylosaurs were lizard-like in body form, but their legs had not yet rotated beneath the body and they moved on land in the same ungainly fashion as did amphibians. All cotylosaurs were extinct by the end of the Triassic but these so-called 'stem reptiles' had, by then, given rise to the ancestors of all of the later reptiles. The turtles may have arisen directly from the cotylosaurs because the earliest known turtle, *Proganochelys*, has many of the characteristics of modern turtles (carapace, toothless jaws and short face to name a few) and the skull is clearly anapsid. The anapsid skull of these early turtles seems not to have been secondarily derived from that of a diapsid ancestor and the concensus now is that the turtles have been around to see virtually all of the rise and fall of the class Reptilia as well as the entire evolutionary histories of birds and mammals. The third anapsid order, the Mesosauria, contains one genus, *Mesosaurus*. This reptile was about 2 ft (60 cm) long and, judging from its limbs and teeth, was an aquatic fish-eater. Its remains have been found in South America and South Africa, a situation which we will have occasion to mention again because mesosaurs were freshwater reptiles, not marine.

The cotylosaurs, in the Middle Permian, gave rise to the first of the lepidosaurs, the eosuchians, which had two temporal openings on each side of the head – the diapsid condition. The living reptile most similar to the early diapsids is the Tuatara *Sphenodon* (order Rhynchocephalia). Although it has been called a 'living fossil', *Sphenodon* itself has been isolated in New Zealand for so long that it is probably quite specialized. In general body form and sprawling gait, however, it probably resembles its Triassic ancestors or at least some of them. A few ancient rhynchocephalians had themselves become highly specialized. These animals, called rhynchosaurs, were more upright in stance and were larger than *Sphenodon*. In addition, rhynchosaurs had bizarre, hooked snouts and unusual dentition. There have been several suggestions as to what these reptiles ate that required such adaptations, including molluscs and hard-shelled fruits, but no one knows for certain.

Rhynchocephalians died out, for the most part, as the archosaurs, including the dinosaurs, gained prominence. Lizards, on the other hand, flourished. Lizards are often thought of as 'modern' reptiles, but they had evolved from eosuchians by at least the Middle Triassic. The diapsid skull condition of lizards is modified in that the bone forming the ventral border of the lower temporal opening is missing. Two primitive lizards are noteworthy because they demonstrate that primitive forms need not be unspecialized. In fact, it may not be fair to consider these two examples as primitive although they lived during the Upper Triassic. *Kuehneosaurus*, from southern England, and *Icarosaurus*, from New Jersey in the United States, had elongate ribs outwardly similar to those seen in the southeast Asian flying lizard, *Draco* (Agamidae) today. These ribs most likely supported a folding membrane which, when expanded, allowed the animals to glide. The most spectacular lizards were the mosasaurs of the Upper Cretaceous. These were huge marine fish-eaters, some reaching a length of 40 ft (12 m), which had elongate bodies and paddle-shaped limbs. The

first great radiation of lizards came to an end in the Jurassic or Lower Cretaceous and gave way to the second radiation, the results of which are apparent today.

The earliest known snakes were Cretaceous in age but snakes may have evolved during the Late Jurassic. It is certain that snakes evolved from lizards, but there has been considerable debate as to which group of lizards was the probable ancestor. There are too few fossil snakes known from the Mesozoic to be of much help and the skull, which is critical in any discussion of snake origins, is rarely well-preserved. The most primitive living snakes have both relatively rigid upper jaws and vestigial pelvic girdles and are mostly burrowers. This has led some investigators to conclude that snakes arose from burrowing lizards with much reduced limbs. Others, emphasizing the marine sediments in which some Cretaceous snake remains have been found, conclude that the first snakes were marine. A third view is held by many herpetologists and paleontologists today, and that is that the snakes arose from lizards of the superfamily Platynota. It is these lizards which most resemble snakes in their anatomy, and they are surface-dwellers with no limb reduction (although most are adept at digging burrows). Anyone unfamiliar with the anatomical arguments for a platynotan origin of snakes would see very little in common between the two groups because platynotans include the monitor lizards (family Varanidae) which are noted for their size, the Gila monster and Beaded lizard (family Helodermatidae) which are heavy-bodied terrestrial or semi-arboreal animals and the only poisonous lizards, and *Lanthanotus* (Lanthanotidae) which is a long-bodied, short-legged, semiaquatic lizard from Borneo. All of these lizards share certain characteristics with snakes: the two halves of the lower jaw are not firmly joined anteriorly, and both vertebral and tongue morphologies are similar. The anatomy of the eye in snakes is quite specialized and some investigators believe that it would have been impossible for it to have been derived from the eye of a non-burrowing lizard, but this objection to a platynotan origin may be dispensed with if we assume that the ancestral platynotans were themselves burrowers.

Although it is assumed that amphisbaenians also evolved from lizards, there is virtually no fossil record to indicate from which group they arose. The earliest records are from the Paleocene of North America.

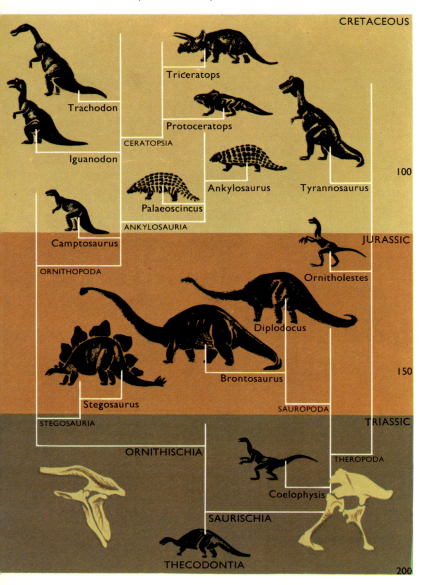

A phylogeny, or 'family tree,' of the dinosaurs, superimposed on a segment of the geological time scale. The numbers represent millions of years before the present. The two major groups of dinosaurs, the Ornithischia and the Saurischia, are depicted; their distinctive pelvic girdles are seen in side view.

Ruling Reptiles. Of all the extinct reptiles, none have captured the imagination of man more than the archosaurs, the 'ruling reptiles'. Included within this subclass are the crocodilians, two groups of dinosaurs, and the pterosaurs. These are diapsid reptiles but most investigators follow Romer in the belief that archosaurs and lepidosaurs evolved the diapsid skull independently. The first archosaurs, the thecodonts, appeared in the Upper Permian and survived well into the Triassic. Their origins are not known with certainty, some paleontologists suggest-

ing an eosuchian ancestor, others a cotylosaur origin. There was a variety of types of thecodont, but all had fore limbs more or less shorter than the hind limbs, and some were capable of bipedal movement, the fore part of the body counterbalanced by a long and heavy tail. One group, the aquatic, fish-eating phytosaurs of the Late Triassic, were very similar to crocodilians but were not derived from them. Phytosaurs were apparently unable to compete successfully with the contemporary crocodilians and were extinct by the Jurassic. The long-term success of the crocodilians has been attributed by several paleontologists to their conservative life-style and morphology. They have changed little since their origins in the Upper Triassic.

The two orders of dinosaurs are distinguished by the structure of the pelvic girdle. In the saurischians the pelvis was triradiate whereas that of the ornithischians was tetraradiate. Not all dinosaurs were giants, several were scarcely a yard in length, but the first discovered dinosaurs were large, the very name dinosaur meaning 'terrible lizard'. The saurischians were the first to appear, in the Middle Triassic. The early saurischians were small carnivores with relatively small heads and long, slender necks. Called coelurosaurs, these dinosaurs were bipedal and probably agile runners, but they were not the real 'terrible lizards' of the time. That honour goes to carnosaurs exemplified by *Allosaurus* and the famous (or notorious) *Tyrannosaurus rex*. These monsters were about 33 and 50 ft (10 and 15 m) long respectively, and may have stood as tall as 20 ft (6 m). They were bipedal with long hind limbs and relatively small and, in *Tyrannosaurus*, bird-like fore limbs. Another group of saurischians were herbivorous but 'terrible' nonetheless. *Brachiosaurus*, a quadrupedal giant probably inhabiting lakes and swamps, measured approximately 79 ft (24 m) from head to tail and may have weighed close to 50 tons.

Ornithischians first appeared in the Upper Triassic, but they were rare until mid-Jurassic. All were herbivorous, some were bipedal, but most were quadrupeds. It is generally accepted that ornithischians evolved from a bipedal ancestor but their ancestry is in doubt. Many of the non-amphibious, quadruped ornithischians were protected by extensive armour. The stegosaurs such as *Stegosaurus* had a double set of upright vertebral plates running from the back of the head well onto the tail. The tail was equipped with heavy pairs of long spikes which were presumably used in active defence against their

Theropoda - *Allosaurus*

Sauropoda - *Cetiosaurus*

Plesiosaur - *Macroplata*

Pterosauria -
Rhamphorynchus

Ornithopoda - *Iguanodon*

Early Thecodont - *Euparkeria*

Ceratopsiae - *Protoceratops*

From a common ancestor like *Euparkeria*, a primitive reptile of the Mesozoic period, there evolved swimming, flying, and terrestrial reptiles that were quadrupedal or bipedal. They also differed in their diet, some becoming fish eaters, others, herbivores or carnivores.

Stegasaurians Ankylosaurs - *Polacanthes*

saurischian relatives. The anklyosaurs carried this one step farther, encasing the entire body in close-fitting plates. These dinosaurs must have looked like giant armadillos! The beaked dinosaurs, the ceratopsians, developed a bony frill at the back of the head where it would have protected the neck. Larger ceratopsians also had horns and *Triceratops*, the one probably best known to the layman, had a horn over each eye and another above the snout. The bipedal ornithischians were not so heavily armoured and

some of these were well-adapted for a semi-aquatic life with webbed feet and nasal passages which travelled through bony crests on the animal's head, thus preventing water from entering the lungs if the head was dunked beneath the water. Ornithischians of this type, because of the shape of the head, were called duck-billed dinosaurs.

Almost as well-known as the dinosaurs to the general public, the pterosaurs represented an unsuccessful attempt to exploit the aerial environment. It is thought that they evolved from arboreal thecodonts, but nothing more specific can be said with certainty. Probably better gliders than flyers, pterosaurs were supported in the air by a membrane stretched between the elongate fourth toe of the fore limb and the body and hind limbs. Their flight apparatus was in fact more similar to that of bats than of birds. Pterosaurs apparently inhabited sea coasts and their long, tooth-studded jaws were beak-like and obviously adapted for catching fish. In primitive forms, the 'beak' was not so long and there was a well-developed tail. More advanced pterosaurs had a much reduced tail, a well-developed beak and a pronounced cranial crest. The hind limbs were too small to support the body upright and it is questionable as to whether pterosaurs could move on land at all. Whereas some pterosaurs were small and delicate, others were true giants. The Cretaceous pterosaur *Pteranodon* had a wingspan of up to 24 ft (7·5 m) and recent discoveries have indicated that much larger forms existed. It is probable that these huge but inefficient reptiles were out-competed by birds and the last records of them are in the Late Cretaceous.

It is widely accepted that, as reptiles, dinosaurs were ectothermic, and it is *almost* unanimously understood that the crocodilians are the only surviving archosaurs, dinosaurs having become extinct at the close of the Cretaceous. The startling suggestion has recently been made, however, that dinosaurs were in fact endothermic ('warm blooded'), some species actually having a hairy coat or feathers! Several lines of evidence support this conclusion, including the observation that the bone structure of dinosaurs is more similar to that of endotherms than of ectotherms. It must be assumed that the 'ectothermic' bone histology of crocodilians was either inherited directly from the early thecodonts or was secondarily derived from endothermic ancestors. As a result of these observations, it has even been suggested that birds, which are endothermic, are in fact dinosaurian – it may be that you have only to look out of your window to see a living dinosaur!

Other Reptilian Types. After surveying the archosaurs, a discussion of the remaining groups of extinct reptiles may seem anticlimactic, but some very unusual groups remain and we have yet to consider that from which mammals arose. Let's turn our attention first to the subclass Euryapsida. These reptiles had a single, dorsal temporal opening. The Araeocelidia were probably terrestrial but had elongate cervical or neck vertebrae similar to those of the marine sauropterygians. The latter had short, wide bodies, flipper-like limbs and long necks terminating in a relatively small head. They were fish-eaters and some, the plesiosaurs, reached lengths close to 48 ft (15 m). Some have suggested that the Loch Ness monster, if it exists, is a plesiosaur. The plesiosaurs are presumed to have been extinct since the Cretaceous. The third order of euryapsids, the Placodontia, was a small group of reptiles specialized as mollusc-eaters. They were heavy-bodied reptiles with long tails and unspecialized limbs, but they

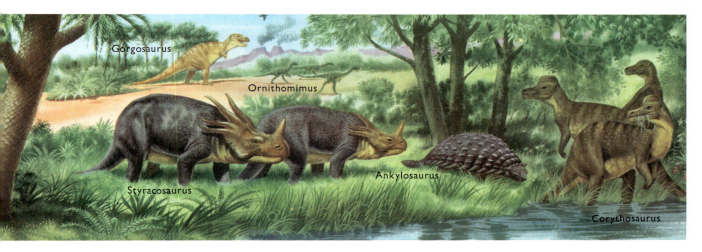

A reconstruction of a Mesozoic scene from 70 to 120 million years ago. During this period, large dinosaurs dominated.

had broad, flat teeth adapted for crushing shells. They showed none of the streamlining evident among the plesiosaurs or the final order of euryapsids, the Ichthyosauria. The ichthyosaurs were, until recently, placed in their own subclass, the Ichthyopterygia, but Romer has argued convincingly, on the basis of well-preserved fossil remains, that ichthyosaurs are euryapsids. These marine reptiles were porpoise-like, with a long snout well equipped with teeth for fish catching (one group had dentition adapted, as in placodonts, for mollusc-eating), paddle-like limbs, a dorsal fin and fish-like tail. Unlike porpoises, however, the vertebral support of the tail was in the ventral lobe. The fortuitous discovery of a fossil ichthyosaur containing a nearly full-term foetus proves that at least some were viviparous. These reptiles were the dominant reptiles of Mesozoic seas, but they disappeared in the Upper Creataceous.

The synapsids, or mammal-like reptiles, are characterized by a single, lateral temporal opening. Two orders are recognized. The pelycosaurs were the commonest reptiles of the early Permian. Several groups (suborders) are recognized. The ophiacodonts were mostly relatively small, amphibious, and lizard-like. Many were adapted for fish-eating. The ophiacodonts gave rise to the carnivorous sphenacodonts and the herbivorous edaphosaurs. The sphenacodont *Dimetrodon*, which reached a length of about 10 ft (3 m), and the edaphosaur *Edaphosaurus* had elongate neural spines on vertebrae which are presumed to have supported a large 'sail'. The function of this sail in these terrestrial reptiles is not known, but it has been suggested that it was a thermoregulatory device rich in blood vessels. When oriented toward the sun, such a 'sail' would have facilitated heat gain, and when the animal moved into the shade, it would have enhanced heat loss. Pelycosaurs were replaced during the Permian by the therapsids which dominated until early in the Triassic. Both herbivorous and carnivorous forms were known, and these reptiles underwent an impressive radiation during the Upper Permian. Therapsids gave rise to mammals in the Upper Triassic and, as many of the characters which distinguish mammals from reptiles are physiological and because other, osteological characters have not been well-preserved in the fossil record, there has been considerable disagreement as to just where to draw the line between the two classes. Advanced therapsids had achieved a number of mammal-like characters including a secondary palate separating the olfactory (nasal) passage from the oral passage, heterodont teeth (having different shapes), two points of articulation between the skull and vertebral column (a characteristic shared with amphibians), and limbs pulled beneath the body lifting it off the ground and permitting more rapid and agile movements. It is not possible to tell exactly when reptiles became endothermic, when hair first appeared and when mammary glands came into being. In other words, we can't tell exactly when reptiles were no longer reptiles, but mammals. A mammalian grade of development may have been achieved more than once by the therapsids, but a discussion of the origin of mammals is outside the range of this book.

The End of the Age of Reptiles. The reptiles were the dominant animals during the Mesozoic, so much so that this era has been termed 'the age of reptiles', but widespread reptilian extinctions occurred near

Triceratops, a giant reptile that became extinct during the Upper Cretaceous period.

the end of the Cretaceous and even the seemingly great diversity of modern forms pales with the knowledge of what has gone before. The dramatic demise of the dinosaurs was paralleled by the disappearance of many other groups of reptiles, including pterosaurs, mosasaurs and several families of more conventional lizards, certain of the crocodilians and even some turtles. There may be no single explanation for the massive die-off and, indeed, several have been put forth, but none has received unanimous support. One of the earliest suggestions sought to implicate some catastrophic geological or climatological event. Although the end of the Cretaceous was a period of considerable geological activity during which continental seas disappeared and mountain ranges developed, the speed with which these events occurred cannot be called frantic and would have had no catastrophic effects on the contemporary reptiles. The climatic changes that took place in some parts of the world and associated with the appearance of new mountain ranges would likewise have come about slowly. But these climatic changes may have had gradual adverse effects on especially the larger reptiles of the day. As ectotherms, the reptiles would not have been able to survive long periods of cold or heat in excess of their normal range of tolerance. To survive, reptiles would have had to move out of areas of climatic adversity in search of regions of more moderate climate. If climatic deterioration was in fact the cause of the Cretaceous extinctions, then we might

expect that representatives of groups other than the crocodilians would have found safety in subtropical or tropical parts of the Cretaceous world and survived into the Cenozoic and possibly beyond. As this is obviously not the case, other explanations must be sought.

One such explanation attributes the extinction of dinosaurs at least to overspecialization. Species which had evolved superb adaptations to environmental conditions of the Lower and mid-Cretaceous may have been genetically incapable of adapting to the changing conditions of the Upper Cretaceous. This might explain the demise of some kinds of Cretaceous reptiles, but does not account for the disappearance of the many unspecialized forms nor the survival of such highly specialized animals as the turtles. And it does not explain the extinction of marine reptiles like the mosasaurs and ichthyosaurs which faced much less drastic environmental adjustments than did their terrestrial relatives. The same fault is apparent in hypotheses that assume changes in the vegetation as the cause of extinction of dinosaurs. One such is that changes in the climate of the time fostered the evolution of plants that herbivorous dinosaurs could not adjust to. As populations of these reptiles diminished there would have followed a decrease in the numbers of the carnivorous forms which fed on their plant-eating cousins. There is some evidence to support this idea in the decrease in the number of herbivorous species in the Upper Cretaceous, but this is countered by the observations of paleontologists indicating no great change in vegetation at that time. In any case, this explanation also fails to explain the extinctions of marine species which had entirely different feeding habits.

Some investigators blame the extinction of dinosaurs on competition with early mammals. If this was so, it must have happened in conjunction with other factors because the early mammals were small and unlikely to offer much of a threat to adult dinosaurs. Mammals, however, are endothermic and may have been able to occupy areas vacated by the large reptiles as the Cretaceous climate degenerated. As the mammalian radiation progressed and larger forms appeared, competition between members of the two groups would have been on more equal grounds. Again, this explanation does not explain marine extinctions, and we are left to conclude that none of the foregoing explanations fully explain the precipitous decline of the reptiles at the end of the Cretaceous.

Reproduction

Reproduction is a fact of life itself. All species must reproduce in order to continue to exist and they must do so at a rate that will guarantee the one for one replacement of at least the females in the population. Given the fact that all species of organisms suffer considerable juvenile (or egg) mortality in their ranks, a single female must usually produce many more eggs or young than the one that, if it survived, would replace her. Most amphibian and reptile species are bisexual. That is, there are two sexes and matings occur between individuals of opposite sex. This may seem an elementary and unnecessary statement but, as we shall see, other patterns are possible. If matings are necessary, there may be the possibility of mistakes, matings between individuals of different species resulting in hybrids and disrupting the integrity of the species. Such matings may, for genetic reasons, result in sterile hybrids, or at least hybrids with reduced reproductive potential, but some lead to fully viable and fertile offspring. In this chapter, we will discuss those aspects of amphibian and reptilian reproductive biology which bear on the number of young produced, in what form they are produced initially (eggs or living young) and those aspects which are important in the sense that they promote 'reproductive isolation' between species.

Eggs. Amphibians and reptiles exhibit three more or less distinctive modes of reproduction. Most are oviparous. That is, eggs are laid and, after an incubation period, hatch into either larvae or miniature replicas of the adult. Amphibian eggs are enclosed, singly or in groups, in a gelatinous material secreted around them as they pass down the oviduct. This material swells upon contact with water and provides some protection for the develop-

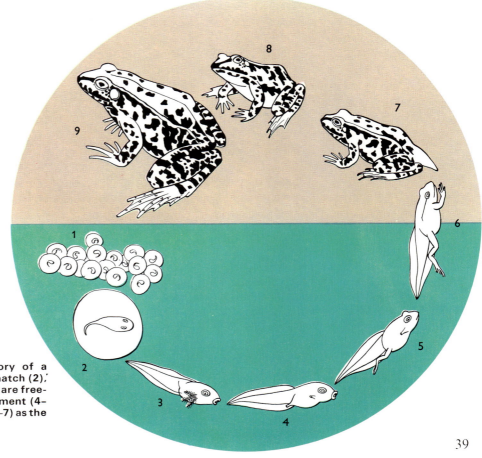

Diagram illustrating the life-history of a typical frog. Eggs laid in water (1) hatch (2), releasing tadpoles (3). The tadpoles are free-living and undergo further development (4–5) culminating in metamorphosis (6–7) as the tadpole becomes a frog (8–9).

39

ing eggs. Yolk nourishes the developing embryo. If the egg is to hatch into a free living larva (frog larvae are often called tadpoles or pollywogs), there may be only a moderate amount of yolk and the eggs may be of the order of one millimetre in diameter. If, on the other hand, there is direct development from egg to miniature adult without a free living, feeding larval stage, the amount of yolk may be relatively large and the egg may be three or four millimetres in diameter as a result.

The eggs of various species of amphibians and reptiles exhibit different time intervals between laying and hatching. This is somewhat temperature-dependent, higher temperatures resulting in more rapid development and consequently shortening the interval between laying and hatching so long as temperatures do not exceed the physiological limits for normal development and survival. Eggs may hatch from hours to months after they are layed. *Sphenodon* (Tuatara) eggs do not hatch until some 13 months after they are laid. Since there is a virtual continuum in time interval between laying and hatching, it should not seem especially surprising that some species retain the eggs within the body until they hatch, the young thereby emerging fully formed albeit small. This mode of reproduction, only arbitrarily distinct from oviparity, is termed ovoviviparity. Eggs are retained within the body through the entire developmental period. Some species are oviparous over part of their range, ovoviviparous in other parts.

In ovoviviparity, there is no direct link between the circulatory systems of the female and the developing young; there is no exchange, or very little, of materials across a membrane, no placenta. The embryo derives most of its food from the parent directly. This mode of reproduction is not common among reptiles and even less so among amphibians. Some authorities believe that viviparity is totally absent among amphibians.

Most amphibians are oviparous and most have free living larval stages. Exceptions are found in each of the living orders, however. The African frog *Nectophrynoides* (Bufonidae) and the Golden coqui of Puerto Rico *Eleutherodactylus jasperi* (Leptodactylidae) are considered ovoviviparous by some authorities, viviparous by others. The same is true of the European fire salamander *Salamandra atra* (Salamandridae) and caecilians of the family Typhlonectidae. Among fire salamanders, a single embryo develops in each oviduct even though more than one egg is present in each. At first, nourish-

ment is derived from the egg yolk. As development occurs, however, the larval salamander eats the yolk of other eggs and eventually develops enlarged gills which contact the highly vascularized walls of the oviduct and through which nutrient materials are passed. Young typhlonectid caecilians apparently derive some nutrients by scraping the uterine walls.

Among the reptiles, the turtles, crocodilians and the Tuatara are wholly oviparous. Most amphisbaenians, lizards and snakes are oviparous as well but many species of amphisbaenians are ovoviviparous and lizards and snakes may be ovoviviparous or viviparous. Although viviparous and ovoviviparous reptiles are widely distributed, high altitude and high latitude faunas harbour a greater proportion of live bearers than do other areas. In cooler climates development may be enhanced by the thermoregulatory behaviour of the parent which can move to warmer areas, something an egg cannot do once laid.

Fertilization. Both internal and external fertilization of eggs is practised among amphibians. This is possible because amphibian eggs are not protected by a shell when laid through which sperm cannot penetrate. Because a tough shell does form around reptilian eggs prior to laying, external fertilization is impossible and sperm must be introduced into the female reproductive tract before the shell forms. Internal fertilization occurs in the Tailed frog *Ascaphus truei* (Leiopelmatidae) and *Nectophrynoides*, all caecilians and all salamanders except members of the families Cryptobranchidae, Hynobiidae, and possibly the Sirenidae. Only Tailed frogs and caecilians have an intromittent organ for transferring sperm from the male into the female. In both, the organ (the 'tail' of the Tailed frog) is an extension of the cloaca, the common chamber into which the reproductive, digestive and urinary tracts empty. Sperm transfer in salamanders is accomplished via a spermatophore, a gelatinous support upon which rests a packet of sperm. Several spermatophores are deposited on the substrate by male salamanders in the course of courtship (see below) and the female picks up the sperm 'cap' with the lips of her cloaca. The sperm are stored in a spermatheca, a chamber inside the cloaca, and eggs are fertilized as they pass by at the time of laying. Egg laying may occur almost immediately, or be delayed for up to several months with the sperm remaining viable in the spermatheca in the interim.

Sperm storage is not limited to salamanders. Seminal receptacles are found in a number of lizards and snakes and viable sperm has been found in the reproductive tracts of female Box turtles *Terrapene carolina* (Emydidae) four years after the last mating. Thus, several clutches of eggs laid over relatively long periods of time may be fertilized by the sperm derived from a single mating. This removes the necessity of a female finding a mate every breeding season to ensure reproduction. A decrease in sperm viability or abundance is, however, observed through time, and in the Diamondback terrapin *Malaclemmys terrapin* (Emydidae) the percentage of eggs fertilized decreased from 99% to 3% over a period of four years.

sufficient to produce the necessary ponds and suitable temperatures. When the proper conditions are met, breeding activity can be explosive. The Spotted salamander *Ambystoma maculatum* (Ambystomatidae) regularly migrates from hibernacula to the breeding ponds during and after the first warm rain following the spring thaw in New England. I have seen literally hundreds of these salamanders crossing a road and ground still covered with a layer of snow and ice in mid-March near Boston. And anyone living in a desert region will be familiar with the almost deafening chorus of frogs and toads which may result from a heavy rain

A Royal python *Python regius* at the moment at which it breaks out of its egg capsule.

The Breeding Season. Whereas amphibians and reptiles in tropical areas with relatively uniform climate and day length throughout the year may not show a cyclic pattern to reproductive activity, there being no seasonality to egg or sperm production, species living in regions exposed to seasonality in temperature or rainfall, or both, demonstrate well defined 'breeding seasons'. Amphibians have been divided into three groups for discussion of factors which initiate breeding activities. One such group characteristically breeds in permanent bodies of water. Non-tropical species breeding in such habitats seem to be influenced most by temperature, whereas tropical species are probably most influenced by rainfall. Temperate zone species in this category are often spring or summer breeders. A second group of amphibians breeds in temporary or semipermanent bodies of water and breeding activities are initiated by a combination of rain

following a long, seasonal drought. Many such breeding aggregations may be composed of several species, all taking advantage of the sudden plethora of precipitation. As the rains may come at different times in different areas, a species may have to adjust its breeding season accordingly. Thus, the Western spadefoot toad *Scaphiopus hammondi* (Pelobatidae) of the southwestern United States breeds in late winter or early spring in California and mid summer in Arizona. A relative, *Scaphiopus holbrooki*, the Eastern spadefoot, breeds any time between late spring and early autumn so long as heavy rains occur when temperatures are above about 50°F (10°C). During such periods, these animals can be found in ponds; they are rarely encountered otherwise. The third group includes a large number of frogs belonging to the families Bufonidae, Hylidae, Leptodactylidae, Microhylidae and Ranidae and *Leiopelma* (Leiopelmatidae) which are fully terrestrial in their breeding habits, along with most genera of lungless salamanders (Plethodontidae). Rainfall appears to be the primary stimulus to breeding with temperature playing an important, but secondary, role. These amphibians lay their eggs in moist places, such as under rocks or in rotting logs, and development is direct; there is no free living larval stage. Many of the species belonging to this category are tropical or live in environments characterized generally by high humidity. With respect to all three groups, although I have emphasized the roles of temperature and rainfall, photoperiod, as expressed by day-length, may be an important determinant of periodicity in breeding. Regardless of how these factors interact to initiate

A European common toad *Bufo Bufo* with its eggs, which are laid in strings.

breeding activities and affect the early stages of egg development, final ripening of the egg is dependent upon interaction between the female and a breeding male during courtship.

Among reptiles, rainfall is, with some exceptions, of less importance than temperature and day length in initiating reproductive activity. This might be expected in as much that reptiles are not as closely tied to environmental water as are amphibians. In general, reptilian reproductive activity is stimulated by increasing day length at appropriate temperatures. For example, the Green anole *Anolis carolinensis* (Iguanidae) of the southeastern United States must be exposed to temperatures of at least 90°F (32°C) during the day before day length affects the reproductive pattern. Reptiles may respond to the slight but regular shifts in day length. Lizards of the genus *Emoia* (Scincidae) in the New Hebrides, where the longest day of the year is less than two hours longer than the shortest, display a good correlation between day length and reproductive patterns. Even in the tropics then, where day length and temperature may be relatively constant, some degree of seasonality may be imposed on reptiles with respect to reproduction. This seasonality may not be expressed as a total cessation of reproductive activity but as peaks in activity when day length is longest. And, in the seasonal tropics where seasons are determined by annual patterns of rainfall, breeding activities may be correlated with rainfall. The relationship here may be somewhat indirect in as much that the rainfall itself may not be of such importance as related changes in the relative abundance of food. The timing of egg laying by the Nile crocodile *Crocodylus niloticus* (Crocodylidae) illustrates another indirect link between rainfall and reproduction. In some parts of its range, the Nile crocodile lays eggs during the dry season which hatch as the rainy season results in flooded rivers and lakes.

Whatever the stimulus that acts to initiate production of eggs or sperm, successful reproduction by most species of amphibians and reptiles requires a meeting of the sexes for the purpose of mating. This simple statement masks a great deal of complex behaviour on the part of the animals. Species of amphibians and reptiles may favour different types of breeding sites and individuals must recognize and find them. Once at the breeding site, individuals must not only recognize members of the same species but also members of the opposite sex. It is these activities that we will now consider.

Breeding in Frogs. No generalities have been drawn concerning the means by which amphibians locate breeding sites. For fully aquatic species such as the Clawed frog *Xenopus laevis* of Africa and its South American relative, the Surinam toad *Pipa pipa* (both members of the family Pipidae), the breeding site may simply be where male meets female. The same may be said of fully terrestrial species of frogs (for example *Hylactophryne*, family Leptodactylidae, from the Mexican plateau) and salamanders (for example lungless salamanders of the genus *Plethodon*, family Plethodontidae). Other species, however, disperse over wide areas outside the breeding season and such species may form large breeding aggregations at suitable sites during the breeding season. Among frogs, call is obviously important in attracting individuals to breeding sites. The first male to arrive attracts both females and other males to the same area. But the call cannot be the only cue drawing frogs to the breeding site or the first male might never have arrived. Nor can call explain how voiceless salamanders are attracted to the sites. A wide variety of cues have been suggested or implicated in attracting amphibians to appropriate breeding sites. Included among these are slope, celestial cues (the use of a sun or star 'compass'), and temperature, humidity, oxygen (for aquatic species) or odour gradients.

Male frogs typically arrive at breeding sites before females, select a calling site and begin to call. The choice of breeding site, calling site and the call itself may all differ among species and act as reproductive isolating mechanisms reducing the chances of hybridization between species. Dr William E. Duellman has provided a series of examples of Middle American tree frogs of the family Hylidae which will serve to illustrate how this works. *Smilisca sordida* breeds in streams, whereas *Hyla ebraccata*, *H. loquax*, *Smilisca baudini*, *S. puma* and *Agalychnis callidryas* are pond breeders. All of the pond breeders were studied in a single pond near Puerto Viejo in Heredia Province of Costa Rica. Calling sites of males of *H. ebraccata*, *H. loquax* and *S. puma* were associated with vegetation in the pond: the small *H. ebraccata* from broad leaves parallel to and about 1 ft (30 cm) above the surface of the water, *H. loquax* from floating logs or large leaves just above the water, and *S. puma* in the water within clumps of dense grass. *Smilisca baudini* calls from ground near the water or while sitting in shallow water and in relatively open sites, and *A. callidryas* calls from trees overhanging the pond.

Nile crocodiles *Crocodylus niloticus* (top) emerge from their eggs. The mother opens the nest to allow the young to crawl out. (Below) an African treefrog *Hyperolius* calling at night, showing the enormous vocal sac.

The calls of all of these species differ in various ways such as in the number of notes per call, the number of notes per minute, and the frequency of the call. It has repeatedly been demonstrated that female frogs are attracted to calling males of their own species and not of other species. Females make the choice of mate and males are rather indiscriminate in trying to mate with any frog that approaches. For this reason, differences in call site are important in that they draw females to sites unoccupied by males of the wrong species. Should a mistake occur, however, and a male attempt to mate with a female of another species, the female may recognize this in the way the male grasps her or in his size or texture. A so-called 'release call' emitted by the female (or a male, should the amorous male be so blind) will cause the offending male to release his hold. A further isolating mechanism involves the site at which the eggs are laid. *Smilisca baudini* lays its eggs over relatively large areas of surface film in shallow water. *Agalychnis callidryas* deposits the eggs in tear-drop shaped clumps on leaves in trees overhanging the water. As the tadpoles hatch, they drop off the leaf into the water below. It is unlikely that a *Smilisca baudini* would climb a tree to fertilize the eggs of an *Agalychnis*, and equally improbable that *Agalychnis* would descend to the water to mate with a female *Smilisca*.

There is no lengthy courtship in frogs. The female is stimulated by the call or presence of the male and allows him to grasp her from above, clasping her with his front legs just behind her front legs or just in front of her hind legs (axillary and inguinal am-plexus, respectively). This positions the cloaca of the male above that of the female and sperm is released over the eggs as they are shed.

Frogs of the family Pipidae mate under water and, in the Surinam toad, the eggs are incubated in the back of the female. Amplexus is inguinal in these frogs. The pair pushes off from the bottom so that they both are upside down, the male beneath the female as eggs are laid, three to five at a time. The eggs are caught on the male's belly. As the pair return to the bottom, they right themselves so that the eggs fall off the male's belly and onto the female's back where they stick and are embedded by pressure from the male. The pair may have been in amplexus for 24–30 hours prior to egg laying and, during that time, the skin of the female's back becomes swollen. After the eggs are implanted in the female's back, further swelling occurs and the eggs become encysted and develop there until they hatch.

Breeding in Salamanders. Among terrestrial salamanders which return to permanent or temporary bodies of water to breed, males customarily arrive first at the breeding site just as was the case in frogs. It is known that certain species of salamanders, such as *Taricha rivulosa* (Salamandridae) of western North America, have considerable homing ability. It is also evident for some species that individuals return to the same breeding site (the one in which they developed?) at every breeding season. Whether homing in involved in this is not known but if so, the animals must have some capacity to retain directional information or use environmental cues following the long period

Left: Male and female toads *Bufo bufo* in amplexus. Right: smooth newts, *Triturus vulgaris* courting. The male (left) develops a crest during the breeding season and vibrates the tail to drive a stream of water at the female.

Two male Warty newts *Triturus cristatus* leave their breeding pond in the autumn at the end of the breeding season.

between breeding seasons. Whatever the mechanism, individuals cannot rely on auditory cues from early arriving males because, with the exception of the Pacific giant salamander *Dicamptodon ensatus* (Ambystomatidae) of the extreme western United States and southwestern Canada, no salamander is known to have a voice. *Dicamptodon* has the ability to produce a low pitched rattling sound if disturbed.

Salamanders of the families Hynobiidae and Cryptobranchidae are not known to exhibit courtship behaviour at all. Males are apparently attracted to females when eggs sacs begin to protrude from the cloaca. For some species it appears that the egg deposition site is selected by the male and there exists the possibility that females are drawn to it by chemical cues provided by the male. External fertilization is the rule in both families with fertilization occurring during or after egg deposition. Males of *Ranodon sibiricus*, a stream-breeding hynobiid, deposit a very sticky spermatophore to which the female attaches the egg cluster. Nothing is known of the courtship of sirens (Sirenidae), but fertilization is assumed to be external. Aside from the three families just discussed, salamanders practise internal fertilization via a spermatophore and have courtship rituals of

varying complexity. The stages of courtship have been systematized and summarized, five distinct stages being recognized.

In stage A, the male becomes aware of the presence of a female, approaches her and often nudges or rubs her with his snout. Stage B involves continued rubbing after the male has ascertained the sex of the female and has either captured her or blocked her from further movement. During this stage, the male may wave his tail about. Stage C, omitted by some species, finds the male moving away from the female with the female following, her attention fixed on some part of his body, often the base of the tail or the cloaca. The spermatophore is deposited in Stage D, and in Stage E the male moves away from the spermatophore followed by the female until the lips of her cloaca contact the sperm cap of the spermatophore. In as much as courtship behaviour in salamanders acts as a reproductive isolating mechanism to discourage hybridization, there is considerable variation, each species displaying characteristic details. We will examine more closely the courtship behaviour of the European newt *Triturus* (Salamandridae) as an example.

In the European newt courtship, stage A is reduced to a touch of the male's snout against the female's cloaca. In stage B the male continually blocks the path of the female by moving in front of her. There is very little contact between the individuals, but the male lashes his tail rhythmically so as to direct a stream of water towards the female's snout. This tail-fanning is thought to direct secretions from the male's cloaca to the female and, as the males are brightly coloured with broadly keeled tails, both visual and olfactory stimuli may be important. At the end of stage B, the male may strike his tail against the female. Stage C consists of the male leading the female forward as she concentrates her attention on his open and brilliantly coloured cloaca. This leads to spermatophore deposition, stage D, which may be stimulated as the female's nose contacts the male's cloaca. The female then picks up the sperm packet, apparently a deliberate move in *Triturus* because the females of most species appear to press the cloaca onto the spermatophore whereas *T. alpestris* females are reported to actively introduce the sperm packet into the cloaca with the hind limbs.

Some salamanders possess glands, called hedonic glands, whose secretions are sex stimulants. Hedonic glands may be located on various parts of the body of a male salamander, but most frequently on the head (for example, the so-called mental gland under the chin) and at the base of the tail. These glands have been most extensively studied and reach their greatest development in the lungless salamanders of the family Plethodontidae. In the plethodontids which have been studied, which include the European grotto salamander *Hydromantes genei* and a wide variety of New World forms, there is always a stage B manoeuvre in which the male rubs the mental gland over the female's snout. This continues into stage C as the male passes beneath the female's chin until her chin comes to rest at the base of his tail whereupon the male leads the female forward, her chin resting at the base of his tail and her legs straddling his tail.

Nothing is known of courtship in caecilians, and we will now turn our attention to reptiles. We will concentrate briefly on turtles, lizards, snakes and crocodilians for lack of knowledge concerning amphisbaenians and the Tuatara. Mention should be made, however, of the interesting fact that the tuatara has no intromittent organ for transfer of sperm from male to female even though reproduction is via eggs and fertilization must be internal.

Breeding in Turtles and Crocodiles. Courtship of turtles has been observed for a number of species and involves both visual and olfactory cues as well as

tactile stimulation of the female by the male. Turtles also demonstrate a number of special adaptations to facilitate mating where both partners are rigidly encased in a shell. Although there are differences in male and female colours in some turtles, such as the presence of red eyes in male Box turtles *Terrapene carolina* (Emydidae) and yellow eyes in females, such variation is not widespread. Visual cues important in sex or species identification are, therefore, in the perception of specific movements rather than colour differences. Only in *Geochelone travancorica* (Testudinidae), an Indian tortoise, are colour changes known to be associated with the breeding season. The courtship of this species and of *G. denticulata* and *G. carbonaria* of South America have been studied. For the South American forms, species recognition is accomplished during the breeding season as a male challenges any other turtle with a series of horizontal head movements. Identical reciprocal head movements by the challenged turtle indicate a male of the same species and leads to an aggressive encounter. Individuals belonging to other species, immature individuals of the same species and females of the same species give no reciprocal response. No response to a challenge causes the challenging male to investigate the cloacal area of the other turtle and recognition of a female of the same species is olfactory. *Geochelone travancorica* accomplishes both species and sex recognition by olfactory means. After recognition, the male attempts to mount the female from behind. This is sometimes preceded by a sort of courtship involving the butting and nipping of the legs of the female which probably serve primarily to immobilize her. Only butting ('shell ramming') is employed by *G. travancorica*. Successful mounting and copulation requires that the female remains immobile for long periods of time. To facilitate mounting, turtles like *Geochelone* and *Terrapene*, which have high-vaulted shells, employ various modifications of the ventral shell (the plastron), the feet and the tail. In *Geochelone*, the plastron of the male is concave, allowing it to fit more snugly over the dorsal shell (the carapace) of the female and providing more than one point of contact. In addition, the tip of the tail of the male has a scale-covered hook which is normally directed toward the ground. When the male mounts the female, however, the tail is turned forwards, beneath and against the plastron of the female and may encounter one of the sutures between the scales of the plastron. This may help the male to remain upright. Similar tail modification is noted in turtles of the family Kinosternidae and in some sea turtles. Both of these groups mate in the water. With the tail turned under, the cloaca of the male lies opposite that of the female and the penis may be inserted. Cloacal position also serves as a reproductive isolating mechanism in that if a male *G. travancorica* mounts a female *G. elegans*, a turtle found in the same area, the cloaca of the male is too far forwards relative to that of the female for copulation to occur.

For comparison, we might compare the courtship of *Geochelone* just discussed with that of the Red-eared turtle *Chrysemys scripta elegans* (Emydidae) of North America. Courtship of this turtle takes

foot of the male being greatly elongate. During titillation, the female closes her eyes and may partially withdraw her head. Finally, the male moves behind the female and mounts. Courtship will be terminated if the proper response is not given at any time during the sequence, as might occur should a male begin to court a female of a different species. The female must, for example, remain essentially immobile for the titillation to be terminated in the proper manner and for copulation to occur.

Information on the breeding biology of crocodilians is largely anecdotal and good data are available only for the Nile crocodile and the American alligator *Alligator mississipiensis* (Alliga-

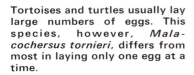

Tortoises and turtles usually lay large numbers of eggs. This species, however, *Malacochersus tornieri*, differs from most in laying only one egg at a time.

place in the water. Courtship behaviour begins as the breeding male appears to restlessly search for a female. If a female is encountered, she gives no visible indication that she recognizes the presence of the male at all and the male begins to follow her, sniffing at her cloaca. The female continues to move, ignoring the male as he moves in front of her, facing her with fore limbs extended. The female stops swimming at this point and the male begins to titillate her by fanning his claws over her head and drumming on her eyes with the tips of the claws. There is marked sexual dimorphism in claw length in these turtles, the three middle claws of each front

toridae). Most courtship occurs in March. It is not known how individuals locate one another nor how sex determination is accomplished, but both may involve olfactory cues. Alligators possess musk glands on the throat and within the opening of the cloaca, and an additional pair of glands along the back, but no odour detectable by man is given off during courtship or mating. Male alligators are capable of producing loud bellows, which may be heard from some distance, and it was long assumed that they did so during courtship. It is now known that they may bellow at any time during the year and in response to other loud noises, even some

A male Cuban anole *Anolis eque-stris*, showing its dewlap extended as in aggressive or courtship displays.

mechanically produced as by the engine of a truck passing nearby. Once a potential mate is located, in whatever manner, the male is the more active in promoting the relationship. Courtship is a slow, and occasionally long, process during which time the male remains with the female, following her both in the water and on land. On land, he lies alongside the female, occasionally stroking her sides with his fore limb. This may go on for up to 17 days before the female will allow the male to move in front of her in the water, butting her throat and blowing streams of bubbles past her cheeks before copulation occurs. Copulation takes place in shallow water, the male and female lying side by side. The female elevates her tail slightly and bends it away from the male so that his penis may be inserted. Actual copulation takes only a few minutes. Observations on captive alligators kept in groups indicate that a male courts successfully only one female per season. What little is known of the courtship of the Nile crocodile parallels that of the American alligator.

Breeding in Lizards and Snakes. Reproductive behaviour of lizards and snakes has been considerably better documented than that of turtles and crocodilians. For lizards, there is considerable dependence of visual cues for both species identification and sex discrimination. Adult males and females of a given species may be differently coloured, and colour changes associated with the breeding season are known. As important, or more

important to many species of lizards, are the species specific movements made by both sexes or by males alone. In one example, *Anolis nebulosus* (Iguanidae), a small relative of the Green anole but from western Mexico, males are territorial, defending an area against encroachment by other adult males of the same species. If another *Anolis* enters his territory, the resident male will, from a distance, give an assertion display. This consists of a specific pattern of head bobs and 'push-ups' coupled with extension of a brightly coloured fold of skin on the throat called a dewlap. If the intruder persists, the assertion display is replaced by a challenge display, another but distinct series of head bobs and push-ups along with the dewlapping. If the intruder is a persistent male, he may respond in kind or flee. If neither retreats during this ritualistic combat, actual fighting may ensue. If, on the other hand, the intruder turns out to be a female resident in the male's territory or from without, or if it is a juvenile individual, it responds to a challenge in a submissive way. If the male is reproductive, this might elicit a courtship performance of rapid head nods interspersed with assertion displays. If the other lizard is a breeding female, she may give an assertion display and 'flag', that is, raise her head and extend the dewlap, sometimes coupling this with tail wagging. The male approaches the female, mounts her from behind gripping the skin of her neck in his mouth. The tail is twisted beneath that of the female

A newt in which the chin and belly is brightly coloured during the breeding season adopts a similar pose to that of the lizard opposite.

so that the cloacas are opposite and copulation, which may last for almost an hour, occurs.

Under certain conditions, courtship behaviour does not appear to occur: the male simply runs up to the female and mounts her. If she is receptive, she remains passive. Such behaviour has been noted in the laboratory for *A. nebulosus*, and I have observed similar behaviour among *A. gingivinus* on Anguilla in the British West Indies. It is therefore possible that courtship is eliminated if the pair are known to one another.

It should be mentioned that the dewlaps of species of *Anolis* living in the same areas are differently coloured, so that species recognition can be made through a combination of the species having different bobbing movements, different push-up patterns, different flagging patterns, and different dewlap colours. All are important, because all *Anolis* are similar to one another in shape although there are size and habitat differences in addition to the behavioural differences.

Colour can be important in sex determination. In the Rainbow lizard *Agama agama* (Agamidae) juveniles are brown, but males develop the ability to change colours when they become sexually mature. The change can be effected quite rapidly and the head becomes bright orange, the body deep blue and the tail blue and orange banded. A territorial male will behave in an aggressive manner toward another male so coloured, but a female will, if sexually

receptive, arch her back and lift her tail. As the male also head bobs, part of the sex determination mechanism for the female may involve recognition of the bob pattern. There are slight differences in the colour patterns of young and adult females, but there is no conclusive evidence as to whether or not the male recognizes these.

It should be apparent by now that odour plays a minor role, if at all, in lizard reproductive behaviour, whereas vision is very important. The opposite seems to be true among snakes. Population densities of most snakes are not nearly so great as they are in many lizards and so snakes may face the same difficulty encountered by some amphibians in finding another snake of the opposite sex to mate with. Male snakes are apparently attracted to females during the breeding season by simply seeing them or by odour. In temperate and subpolar regions, many snake species hibernate in communal dens. As all the snakes in a den emerge at almost the same time in the spring and breed almost immediately, there is no difficulty in locating a mate. A single den may, however, be used by several species, Prairie rattlesnakes *Crotalus viridis* (Viperidae) and Desert striped whipsnakes *Masticophis taeniatus* (Colubridae) for example, and as these emerge at the same time in the spring, there must be some mechanism for species recognition. This must be accomplished initially by odour. Among non-denning snakes, it has been demonstrated that a

49

male will follow a scent trail left by skin from the back of a female. That odour is important is amply demonstrated by the fact that a male snake having its nostrils plugged or the tips of its tongue removed (the tongue is also used to 'smell' odours) does not court, even in the presence of receptive females. Once a male snake finds a breeding female, he usually follows her, coming up alongside or over her from the back, rubbing his chin against her while tongue-flicking over her skin. The male eventually attempts to twist the hind part of his body around the female's so that his cloaca lies next to hers. Various means are then employed to further stimulate the female. Among boids, which retain external vestiges of the hind limbs, these are scratched against the sides of the female. In other snakes, the male may undulate or jerk his body against the female. In a few species, the male may, as in lizards, grasp the neck of the female in his mouth. All of this activity apparently prompts the receptive female to allow the male to insert one of his two intromittent organs, a hemipenis, into her cloaca. Once copulation begins, it may continue for at least an hour. Touch is important in stimulating the male as well in some species. In the North American garter snakes of the genus *Thamnophis* (Colubridae), for example, males have pressure sensitive scale organs beneath the scales of the chin and these are apparently stimulated as the male rubs his chin along the back of the female. If these organs are artificially covered in some manner, the male will not court. The relative unimportance of visual cues in snake courtship is indirectly indicated by the fact that sexual differences in colour do not occur whereas they are conspicuous along lizards.

Both lizards and snakes have hemipenes. Unlike a true penis, the hemipenis is not a hollow tube but a sac-like structure with a groove, the *sulcus spermaticus* serving as the pathway through which sperm are ejected. The hemipenis has no erectile tissue and is erected by eversion like the inverted finger of a rubber glove as one blows into it forcefully. When not everted, the hemipenes lie beneath the skin behind the cloaca. Eversion is accomplished by the combination of muscular action and inflation of sinuses in the hemipenis with blood. Only one hemipenis is used in copulation. The hemipenes are usually ornamented with a bewildering array of folds, flounces or spines, or a combination of these, and the presence or absence of certain of these and their arrangement is species specific. As such, the hemipenis may serve as another reproductive

isolating mechanism. Differences in structure resulting in incompatability between the hemipenis and the cloaca of the female may render hybridization impossible.

Eggs. The number of eggs or living young produced by a species or by any given female of a particular species is determined by a number of factors. Within a species, the size (and, therefore, age for many species) of the female affects egg production. For example, female Side-blotched lizards *Uta stansburiana* (Iguanidae) measuring $15\frac{3}{4}$–$17\frac{1}{4}$ in (40–44 mm) in body length had mean clutch sizes of 3.48 eggs, whereas females of $19\frac{1}{2}$–$21\frac{1}{4}$ in (50–54 mm) body length had clutch sizes averaging 4.37 eggs. If we compare species, we often find that species utilizing external fertilization produce greater numbers of eggs per clutch than those employing internal fertilization. Thus the Tailed frog *Ascaphus* produces 28–50 eggs per clutch whereas the Eastern spadefoot *Scaphiopus holbrooki* produces 1,000–2,500 and the American toad *Bufo americanus* (Bufonidae) 4,000–8,000. The advantage of internal fertilization lies in the fact that there is less wastage of sperm and higher probability of fertilization for an egg than if sperm is simply deposited over freshly laid eggs in water. An organism that employs internal fertilization can 'afford' to have fewer eggs per clutch because there is a high probability that most or all will be fertilized. Those species which have eliminated a larval stage in their life cycle and in which all development occurs in the egg, which is heavily yolked and relatively large, lay fewer eggs than species which retain a free-living larva. An extreme example is the Cuban frog *Sminthillus limbatus* (Leptodactylidae) which lays only one large, heavily yolked egg at a time although it may produce more than one egg a year. A final factor which affects clutch size is the degree of parental care exhibited by the parent or parents. We will consider this in some depth below, but it should be mentioned that anything which increases the survival probabilities of the young decreases the number of young which must be produced to guarantee replacement of the parents. Of course, parental care imposes a cost on the parents because they may be more subject to, for example, predation themselves while protecting their young.

Parental Care. Parental care is exhibited in one form or another by many amphibians and reptiles. The simplest form of parental care might be the construction of a nest in which to deposit the eggs. Most frogs lay their eggs in water or on land with no attempt to build a nest, but some species of the families Myobatrachidae (Australo-Papuan region), Leptodactylidae (Latin America) and Ranidae (Old World tree frogs sometimes placed in their own family, the Rhacophoridae) build foam nests in which to lay their eggs. Eggs of the Australian frog *Heleioporus* are layed in a foam nest on land, but hatching is delayed until the area in which the nest is placed is flooded and the tadpoles develop in the water. Another Australian frog, *Adelotus*, deposits its eggs in a foam nest produced as the female uses her hands to churn a mixture of mucous and water to trap air bubbles. Females of species which exhibit this behaviour have broad, fleshy flanges on the inner fingers. The leptodactylid *Physalaemus pustulosus* also builds a foam nest, but the male kicks up the mixture of water and mucous. Another type of nest is constructed by the large Latin American tree frog *Hyla boans* (Hylidae). Large, circular nests of sand and gravel are constructed at the edge of streams and the eggs deposited in these. It seems that these nests are used more than once because both eggs and tadpoles have been found in the same nest. Such nests, filled with seepage water or by rains, might serve two purposes. The warming action of the sun might make these nests in effect 'incubators' because water temperatures would be higher than in the adjacent stream and larval development would be enhanced. Also, the many potential egg and tadpole predators found in tropical streams would be absent in the nests, reducing egg and larval mortality. Nests are known for both aquatic and terrestrial species of salamanders. Male Hellbenders *Cryptobranchus alleganiensis* (Cryptobranchidae) hollow out areas under rocks or logs in the water to which females are attracted for egg deposition and subsequent fertilization. The Dusky salamander *Desmognathus fuscus* (Plethodontidae) and its relatives also hollow out an area under a rock, but on land. Both turtles and crocodilians deposit their eggs in nests. These may only be holes dug in sand or soil, but some crocodilians, including the African sharp-nosed crocodile *Crocodylus cataphractus*, New Guinea crocodile *C. novaeguineae*, Estuarine crocodile *C. porosus*, the African dwarf crocodiles *Osteolaemus tetraspis* and *O. osborni*, the American alligator and other members of the family Alligatoridae, and False gavial *Tomistoma schlegeli*, build a so-called 'mound nest' out of plant debris and mud or sand. In the American alligator, the female, using the sides of her body and her tail, scrapes material into a large pile 18–30 in (45–75 cm)

high and 4–5 ft (1·2–1·5 m) in diameter. She moves over this, packing it down, and then digs a cavity in the top with her hind feet. All of this may be done over a span of two or three days and eggs are layed in the cavity soon after the nest is completed. After laying, she crawls over the top of the nest, closing in the cavity. Nests as extensive as this are unknown among other reptiles although most lizards dig a nest hole of some type if they lay their eggs on the ground. The Flap-necked chameleon *Chamaeleo dilepis* (Chamaeleontidae) does, however, cover the earth over the nest hole with vegetation. The King cobra *Ophiophagus hannah* (Elapidae), is the only snake known to construct a nest of plant materials. A female King cobra has been observed to gather leaves, bamboo stalks and sand into a pile using coils of her body, excavate an egg chamber in the middle by coiling and revolving her body, and then cover the eggs after they were laid. Some other snakes lay their eggs in burrows or tunnels, but nest building is not widely practised. Eggs are simply laid in rock piles, under rocks, under and in logs, in leaf litter and so on.

Parental care in some amphibians and reptiles involves brooding the eggs and, in a few species, care of the young to some degree after they are hatched or born. Parental care is well developed among lungless salamanders of the family Plethodontidae where it is apparently necessary for the survival of the clutch. Unattended eggs quickly develop a thick coating of fungus which prevents normal gas exchange between the developing embryo and its environment. In plethodontids of the genus *Desmognathus* egg clutches are attached by stalks, either individually or in groups, to the undersides of rocks or logs in a nest cavity occupied by the female. With the exception of *D. wrighti*, which has direct development, the eggs of these salamanders hatch into aquatic larvae and the eggs of all species may be laid in streamside areas. Apparently the females remain with the eggs from laying to hatching, never leaving even to forage for food although they may eat small organisms that enter the nest cavity. Female Marbled salamanders *Ambystoma opacum* (Ambystomatidae) lay their eggs in low areas on land and curl about them until the area is flooded and the eggs hatch into free-living larvae. The South African bullfrog *Pyxicephalus adspersus* (Ranidae) and the Hellbender are both known to guard eggs and in both cases the male does the job. In the case of the bullfrog this extends past hatching into the tadpole stage of the young. No turtles are known to brood or

A Royal python *Python regius* hatching (below) and leaving the egg (right).

guard their eggs but crocodilians are known to do so as has been well documented for both the Nile crocodile and the American alligator. Lizards of the genera *Ophisaurus* (slow worms or glass 'snakes', family Anguidae) and *Eumeces* (skinks, family Scincidae) brood their eggs and skinks will defend the clutch against such possible predators as mice. Some investigators believe that skinks help to incubate the eggs by basking and then returning to the eggs which absorb some of the heat. In *Ophisaurus* and *Eumeces*, females brood the eggs. Few snakes are known to brood their eggs, although the female King cobra does, as do some other cobras and pythons. Brooding female Burmese pythons *Python molurus bivittatus* (Boidae) coil about their eggs and cap the coil with the head. They are able by metabolic means to elevate the body temperature somewhat above that of the surrounding environment as the eggs are incubated.

Some frogs actually carry the eggs or tadpoles around with them, an extreme in parental care among amphibians and reptiles. You will remember in our discussion of the Surinam toad *Pipa pipa* that the eggs became encysted in the back of the female. They remain there throughout the development of the larva and the young emerge fully formed, miniatures of the adult. This is seen also in the hylid frog *Hemiphractus*. Several hylid frogs carry their young on their backs. This is most advanced in the marsupial frogs of the genus *Gastrotheca* of South America. Females possess a brood sac in which the eggs develop. The sac opens to the outside through a small opening above the cloaca and it is not known how the eggs are deposited in the chamber. The young either leave the sac after hatching as tadpoles or complete their development in the sac. The Midwife toad *Alytes obstetricans* (Discoglossidae) is so named because the male carries the two strings of eggs produced by the female around with him until they hatch. After the strings are laid and fertilized, the male extends his hind limbs backward until the eggs are wound around the posterior part of his body. The eggs, moistened by dew or water into which the male moves, are carried about until they are ready to hatch, at which time the male moves to a pool of water so that the tadpoles will hatch into the environment in which further development will take place. In the genera *Colostethus*, *Dendrobatus* and *Phyllobates* (all Dendrobatidae) males and sometimes females carry tadpoles which adhere to their backs after hatching on land. In *Phyllobates flotator*, for example, young tadpoles have ventrally-placed suctorial mouths which are used to hold the tadpoles to the back of the adult. When they reach an advanced stage of development, they drop off into any water the adult happens to enter. The mouth then becomes dorsal in position, an adaptation for hiding beneath rocks in the water. The frog

Hylambates brevirostris (Ranidae) and Darwin's frog *Rhinoderma darwini* (Rhinodermatidae) have the most bizarre forms of parental care evident among amphibians. *Hylambates* females brood the fertilized eggs in their mouths until they hatch as miniature frogs. The female does not eat during the entire time necessary for this to occur. *Rhinoderma* eggs are laid on land. When the larvae are about to hatch out, their movements stimulate the males (several may gather around one clutch) to pick the eggs up in their mouths and push them into the vocal pouch with the tongue. Each male picks up several eggs which hatch and develop to metamorphosis in the large vocal pouch. When the larvae metamorphose, the young frogs exit via the mouth.

Among lizards, few species exhibit any care for the young after they are hatched or born. The Great plains skink *Eumeces obsoletus* (Scincidae), and perhaps other members of this genus as well, help the young emerge from the egg, and the live-bearing Yucca night lizard *Xantusia vigilis* (Xantusiidae) helps the new-born young to free themselves from the foetal membrane that they are born in. Nothing similar is known for snakes. Very recently well-developed maternal behaviour has been demonstrated for the Nile crocodile. Such behaviour had been rumoured for years with reference to several species of crocodilians, but never documented. Nile crocodiles are hole nesters. When the young crocodiles are about ready to hatch, after an incubation time of about 90 days, they croak from within the eggs. The female then opens the nest and, one at a time, carries each egg to the water, rolling it against the roof of her mouth to break the shell. The little crocodile is released into the water and the performance repeated until all the eggs (up to about 60 of them) have been hatched. The parent or parents remain near the young and the young emit a distress call if molested to bring the parents to their defence.

We will close our discussion of the reproductive biology of amphibians and reptiles with two 'special cases'. The first of these involves the attainment of reproductive maturity in otherwise immature amphibians, the second concerns species of amphibians and reptiles which are unisexual, all or most individuals being females.

Neoteny. Several families of salamanders are considered permanently larval (Amphiumidae, Cryptobranchidae, Necturidae, Proteidae and Sirenidae) and several other families contain species which are not known to metamorphose in nature or species in which some populations or individuals have extended larval lives. The retention of larval characteristics for long periods is known as neoteny; the reproduction of such larval forms is termed paedogenesis. The five families listed above are both neotenic and paedogenic. The phenomenon of paedogenesis is known only in salamanders, but neotenic frogs have been described. Metamorphosis is controlled by the thyroid gland which produces the hormone thyroxine. Many of the paedogenic salamanders in the families Ambystomatidae, Hynobiidae, Plethodontidae, and Salamandridae can be induced to metamorphose if treated with thyroxine. This is not effective on the five permanently aquatic and neotenic families listed above. Among those species with only some populations paedogenic, certain environmental conditions are correlated with the condition. Many are high altitude inhabitants and it has been suggested that the low temperatures encountered there inhibit production of thyroxin and prevent metamorphosis. Ponds with low levels of iodine might also promote neoteny in salamanders inhabiting them because iodine is required for the normal production of thyroxine. In the case of high altitude, subterranean or dry environments, natural selection might favour the ability of a salamander to remain aquatic, to postpone or eliminate metamorphosis. In such

Alpine newts *Triturus alpestris* normally metamorphose, but display retarded development and neoteny in populations found in the cold waters of high level lakes.

The axolotl is a neotenic larval form of the Mexican salamander *Ambystoma mexicanum* (top). If it metamorphoses, it loses its external gills and becomes darker in colour (bottom).

environments, an individual forced to become terrestrial would be at a disadvantage. In some cases, a degree of flexibility is desirable also. If the pond in which a paedogenic population of *Ambystoma tigrinum* (Ambystomatidae) is living begins to dry up, the larvae begin to metamorphose. The advantage of this is obvious: the aquatic habitat is disappearing and extinction is certain if metamorphosis does not occur, possibly less so if it does. No conscious act on the part of the salamanders is implied. Increased crowding of the larvae and an increase in the salt concentration of the water as it evaporates might induce metamorphosis.

Parthenogenesis. Essentially all-female populations are known among both amphibians and reptiles. In such populations, reproduction occurs via unfertilized eggs. This is termed parthenogenesis and is known in the salamander family Ambysto-

matidae and the lizard families Agamidae, Gekkonidae, Lacertidae and Teiidae and is suspected in *Brooksia spectrum affinis* (Chamaeleontidae) from the Ituri Forest, Republic of the Congo. The phenomenon has been most extensively studied for the parthenogenetic species of the teiid lizard genus *Cnemidophorus* (the racerunners), the lacertid genus *Lacerta* (lacertas), and the ambystomatid genus *Ambystoma*. Most parthenogenetic species seem to have arisen through hybridization between two normal, bisexual species at a time when environmental circumstances permitted survival of the hybrids. The eggs of parthenogenetic species require stimulation for development provided by penetration by sperm from one of the parent bisexual species, but the sperm nucleus does not fuse with the egg nucleus to effect a fertilization, and the sperm eventually disintegrates. Parthenogenesis of this type is termed gynogenesis. Populations of parthenogenetic species do occur in the apparent absence of their bisexual 'hosts', and gynogenesis may have been supplanted by full parthenogenesis in these populations.

Parthenogenetic species often occur in habitats that are either more extreme than those occupied by bisexual relatives, or in areas that have a history of glacial or geological disturbance. Unisexual *Ambystoma*, for example, occur in the region of the southern extreme to which Pleistocene glaciation extended into what is now the United States. Unisexual species of *Lacerta* in the southern Caucasus inhabit areas either drier or wetter or both than do the putative parental species although one, *L. dahli*, occurs in environments intermediate to the probable parental species (*L. portshinskii* and *L. mixta*). Research on parthenogenesis in *Lacerta* has suggested that the unisexual species may have arisen 7,000–5,000 years ago when the world was experiencing a relatively arid period, the hypsithermal. Hybrids formed at that time would have been adapted to these drier conditions but (by virtue of the fact that parthenogenetically produced individuals display less variation and therefore form less flexible populations) they would have been unable to occupy more humid habitats as conditions changed over time to what they are today. Bisexual populations, however, are more flexible and have inhabited more moist areas but are out-competed in more arid environments by the unisexual forms. Other hypotheses have been suggested, but all involve a habitat difference between unisexual species and their putative parental species.

Growth, Development and Longevity

We have already introduced the subjects of growth and development as we discussed parental care among amphibians and reptiles in the previous chapter. We now will consider other aspects of these topics, especially as they relate to amphibian larvae and the process of metamorphosis, growth rates of amphibians and reptiles, sizes and ages at which sexual maturity is reached, and longevity of amphibians and reptiles.

Considering the large numbers of amphibian and reptile species, there is surprisingly little information on the length of incubation of eggs or, for live-bearers, gestation period. Much of the information that is available is derived from specimens maintained in captivity and little has been done to relate incubation or gestation times to environmental factors other than laboratory studies with temperature. As considerable variation is exhibited within a single species, it is probable that extrinsic factors are important in determining these time intervals. Among temperate or subpolar zone species, eggs usually hatch or young are born during the same season that fertilization occurs.

Some interesting facts are hidden in the tabular presentation of incubation or gestation periods for amphibian and reptile species given here. Among the toads, the species which lay their eggs in temporary bodies of water, especially in desert regions, such as the Western spadefoot, have very rapid incubation periods. Pond breeding frogs, such as the Bullfrog, have intermediate incubation periods, and the Tailed frog, which lays its eggs in cold mountain streams, has a very long incubation time. The Mexican white-lipped frog lays its eggs in a foam nest at the onset of heavy rains in the arid parts of Mexico in which it lives. The nests are built next to depressions that will fill with water, but mating and egg deposition occur before any standing water exists. The foam nest gives the frogs a head start over other species which may breed in the temporary pond but which must wait until standing water accumulates before doing so. Eggs of several species may overwinter before hatching. This is true for the Painted turtle and the Tuatara. Embryonic development presumably ceases or nearly ceases during the cooler months. Remember that the Garter snake

and the Rattlesnake are live-bearers and the seemingly long gestation times terminate in the birth of a young snake rather than an egg or larval form which must develop further before attaining adult form (if not size).

The importance of temperature in early frog development can be seen in data available for the Grass frog *Rana pipiens* (Ranidae). At 64°F (18°C) hatching took place at about 6 days, metamorphosis at about 90 days. At 76°F (25°C) these times are 5 days and 75 days, respectively. These data are, of course, from laboratory studies and Grass frog eggs and tadpoles in nature would not face constant temperatures.

Tadpoles and Larvae. Upon hatching, frog tadpoles and salamander larvae differ considerably from one another and these differences are magnified as development proceeds toward metamorphosis. The body, exclusive of the tail, is relatively short in tadpoles, long in larvae. Tadpoles have a relatively small but quite complex mouth throughout development whereas larvae develop a rela-

---

Incubation or gestation periods for selected amphibian and reptile species.

Tailed frog *Ascaphus truei* (Leiopelmatidae)	**30 days**
Western spadefoot *Scaphiopus holbrooki* (Pelobatidae)	**2–7 days**
Mexican white-lipped frog *Leptodactylus labialis* (Leptodactylidae)	**1–3 days**
Bullfrog *Rana catesbeiana* (Ranidae)	**5–20 days**
Painted turtle *Chrysemys picta* (Emydidae)	**63–84 days**
Garter snake *Thamnophis sirtalis* (Colubridae)	**90–120 days**
Rattlesnake *Crotalus viridis*	**90–120 days**

tively larger mouth of a more conventional nature. Most tadpoles are herbivorous and the unique oral apparatus is designed to scrape material from plants or algae from the surfaces of rocks, sticks and the like. Salamander larvae, on the other hand, are carnivorous, eating small insects and other invertebrates. Tadpoles initially have two pairs of well-developed external gills, but these become covered by an operculum as the tadpole develops. Water drawn in through the mouth passes over the gills beneath the operculum and passes out of the gill chamber through one or two openings called spiracles. Larvae retain three well-developed external gills to metamorphosis and the operculum, though present, is open and hangs loosely along the side of the neck. Some species of salamanders have larvae with a pair of rods called balancers below the eye on each side of the head; these are lacking in tadpoles. Tadpoles have, at hatching, one or a pair of adhesive organs beneath the head and these are lacking in salamander larvae. Adhesive organs do not persist very long and serve to allow the tadpole to adhere to vegetation or other surfaces before the mouth becomes functional and powers of locomotion develop. Tadpoles do not develop limbs until relatively late in larval life. The slow development of the hind limbs is visible, but the anterior limb buds develop beneath the operculum and the fore limbs appear only at metamorphosis. Salamander larvae are often hatched with well-developed limbs and, with a mouth similar to that of an adult, resemble the adult salamander much more so than a tadpole resembles an adult frog.

Just as adult amphibians demonstrate adaptive radiation in response to opportunities offered by the habitats in which they live, amphibian larvae show adaptations to various environments. Three basic types of salamander larvae are recognized and these are correlated with habitat as first pointed out by G. K. Noble in 1931. Terrestrial breeding salamander larvae lack tail fins, have a large yolk sac which would impede or totally prevent movement were the larvae free-living, and large, branched gills which are spread against the egg membrane where they function as a major component of the larval respiratory system. The larvae of pond-breeding salamanders also have well-developed gills as the environment in which they live may be oxygen-deficient. The larvae have well-developed tail fins which may extend up onto the back. In still water the tail is the primary means of propulsion while swimming and, being well vascularized, serves as a respiratory surface as well. Larvae which develop in swift waters have reduced tail fins and relatively short limbs. They make no attempt to swim against strong currents but move along the bottom among rocks well away from the full force of the current. Long limbs and a large tail fin would be counterproductive in that they would catch the current. In these highly oxygenated waters, gills are also reduced.

Of the permanently neotenic salamanders, gills are retained in the sirens, olms and mud puppies, but are lost in adult Hellbenders and Congo eels. All of these salamanders develop lungs to complement the gills and cutaneous (skin) surfaces in respiration.

Tadpoles show a greater diversity in morphology than do salamander larvae, reflecting the wider variety of habitats in which they are found. Seven different tadpole types have long been identified primarily by general morphology, size of tail fin, and position and structure of the mouth. This is an ecological classification and similar tadpole types can be found in widely divergent frog families. The generalized tadpole type, as exemplified by that of the Grass frog *Rana pipiens* is moderately deep bodied with a large tail fin and a downward-facing mouth adapted for feeding on plants. The nektonic tadpole is a deep bodied form with a relatively large tail fin and no special modification of the mouth. It is adapted for life in open water. The Barking treefrog *Hyla gratiosa* and the Red-eyed hylids *Agalychnis callidryas*, for example, have nektonic tadpoles. Some pond tadpoles are adapted for feeding off the surface of the water by having upwardly facing mouths and the ventral tail fin enlarged in a way that keeps them positioned upward. *Phyllobates flotator* (Dendrobatidae) has this type of tadpole. Some frogs lay their eggs in water-filled holes in trees or in water that collects at the leaf bases of tropical trees and plants. The tadpoles of these frogs, exemplified by *Hyla bromeliacia*, have little need for swimming and the tail fin is greatly reduced. The body may be flattened or otherwise streamlined as well. Some frogs with arboreal tadpole types as just described have adapted to a carnivorous habit which is very unusual among tadpoles. The carnivorous tadpole type is just like the arboreal type, but the mouthparts are modified for eating frog eggs or other tadpoles. *Hyla zeteki* has such a carnivorous, arboreal tadpole and it might be noted that this frog lays its eggs on the leaves of plants called bromeliads above water level, thereby reducing egg cannibalism. Carnivorous tadpoles are found in other habitats as well.

The Mud puppy *Necturus maculosus* retains external gills throughout life, evidence that it is permanently neotenic.

The Eastern spadefoot *Scaphiopus holbrooki* has a pond type carnivorous tadpole. Tadpoles living in fast-flowing mountain streams have reduced tail fins, moderate body size, large suctorial mouths and sometimes an adhesive disc on the lower side of the body. The Tailed frog *Ascaphus truei* has this type of tadpole. The final tadpole type is that associated with direct development and it is generally similar to the larvae of salamanders with direct development. Finally, mention should be made of tadpoles which develop in pockets or pouches of the parent. These tadpoles develop very large gills which may almost enclose the tadpole and which are highly vascularized. They are tightly pressed against the chamber in which the tadpole is developing which is itself vascularized, and the larva thus obtains most of its oxygen from the walls of its chamber.

Duration of larval life in amphibians is dependent on temperature and variation occurs both between species and between members of a single species as was the case with incubation times. Similarly also, tadpoles and larvae of species which breed in temporary bodies of water is relatively short. Thus, Western spadefoot tadpoles have been known to metamorphose only 12–13 days after the eggs were laid. The American Bullfrog, a pond breeder, spends 14 to 16 months as a tadpole in the southern United States. Faced with a shorter 'season' and cooler temperatures in the northern part of its range, however, the bullfrog may not metamorphose until after its third winter. Factors other than temperature that are known to affect duration of larval life and onset of metamorphosis include overcrowding, food availability, and chemical changes in the water in which the larvae are living. Considerable research remains to be done on this subject, however, and there are still many unanswered questions.

Metamorphosis. Amphibians, with the exception of those with direct development and neotenic forms, spend part of their lives as fully aquatic larvae and then, over a very short period of time, are transformed into quite different adults which are usually semiaquatic or primarily terrestrial. Certain larval organs, structures and physiological processes are lost, whereas others are modified for use in the adult. Entirely new organs and processes appear. Amphibians which undergo metamorphosis must have some genes and gene complexes which function only during the larval phase of the life cycle, others which are functional only at the time of metamorphosis, still others specific in action to the adult, and yet more that function throughout life. It should be

Metamorphosis in newts and salamanders, such as this Palmate newt *Triturus helveticus*, is less profound than in frogs. Evidence for this is seen in the retention of the tail.

obvious that the timing of metamorphosis may be critical to the survival of the individual. The Spadefoot unable to transform quickly enough may die as the temporary pool in which it lives dries up. Amphibians at the time of transformation may be especially subject to predation, so there is pressure to complete metamorphosis from larva to adult as rapidly· as possible. The changes attendant on metamorphosis are radical, although more so for frogs which have adults so different from tadpoles than for salamanders whose larvae are similar in many respects to the adults. This is not the forum for a detailed discussion of the hormonal control of metamorphosis, but we will consider the major changes that are associated with the transformation. As frog metamorphosis is more dramatic and radical, we will consider it first, using the North American Grass frog *Rana pipiens* as our example.

Metamorphic Changes. Developmental changes occur uninterrupted from fertilization through the embryonic period (8 days at 74°F (23°C)), a premetamorphic or larval period (35–42 days at 74°F (23°C)) and metamorphosis (28 days at 74°F (23°C)). The metamorphosis stage is customarily divided into a three week prometamorphosis, during which time changes are rather inconspicuous, and a one week metamorphic climax during which major and obvious changes occur which culminate in attainment of adult form and function by the frog. Probably the most apparent changes over this period are the development of the limbs and the loss of the tail. The requirement for limbs by the adult requires no further discussion. As they develop, the hind limbs are visible throughout, but the fore limbs

develop beneath the operculum and degeneration of a corner of the operculum allows them to break through. This action marks the beginning of the metamorphic climax. The limbs are fully developed and functional before the frog actually begins to leave the water, but the tail does not completely degenerate until after. Amphibian larvae usually have developed lungs but these finally become functional during the metamorphic climax as the gills and remainder of the operculum are resorbed. As the changeover from gill breathing to lung breathing occurs, the tadpole begins to gulp air at the surface of the water. Also during the metamorphic climax, the relatively small mouth of the tadpole becomes the wide mouth of the adult. The horny 'teeth' used by the tadpole to scrape vegetation are lost, the adult jaw appears and the tongue more than doubles in length. The long, coiled gut of the herbivorous tadpole shortens because the adult is carnivorous, feeding on insects and other invertebrates for the most part. Changes in the sense organs occur also. The lateral line system in the skin, which is used to detect vibrations through water, is replaced by a system for detecting vibrations that travel through air: the middle ear, tympanic membrane (external 'ear drum') and associated structures. Olfactory organs develop for use in air, and there develop some of the accessory structures to the eye made necessary by a partially terrestrial existence. Lacrimal (tear) glands and ducts form to moisten the eye, and eyelids develop both to protect the eye and as they sweep over the cornea, clean it and spread moisture from the lacrimal gland and oil from another newly developed gland, the harderian gland. The skin is modified for a more terrestrial existence and some blood vessels degenerate. Physiological changes occur as well. The tadpole excretes its nitrogenous waste materials in the form of ammonia, a very toxic but water-soluble substance. A large build-up of ammonia in the organism would be lethal, but water is plentiful for a tadpole and ammonia is excreted as it is formed and not stored. The terrestrial adult may find water in short supply and the excretion of ammonia would require the regular loss of water the animal may not be able to afford to lose. Adult semiaquatic and terrestrial frogs rids themselves of nitrogenous wastes in the form of urea (or, rarely, uric acid): less water-soluble, less toxic and excreted with less loss of water. At metamorphic climax, there is a sudden increase in the production of the enzymes necessary for urea synthesis. These enzymes are produced by the liver. The tadpoles are said to be ammoniotelic, the adults primarily ureotelic.

Some of the metamorphic changes noted in the Grass frog and other semiaquatic or terrestrial frogs do not occur in species where the adults remain fully aquatic. The Clawed frog *Xenopus laevis* (Pipidae), for example, retains the lateral line system for detecting underwater vibrations and remains ammoniotelic.

Metamorphosis in salamanders is much less dramatic than in frogs; the changes are more subtle. The gills may be lost as is the tail fin, and there are changes in the skin and circulatory system, but body form does not change radically and the limbs remain the same. These changes occur over a short period of time, often just a few days, rather than gradually over a long period.

Once amphibians have metamorphosed, growth and the attainment of sexual maturity are the only remaining changes that occur. Young, newly-metamorphosed amphibians are usually similar to the adults even in colour and pattern, but this is not always true if newly hatched or born reptiles are compared with the adults.

Adult Size. Different species of amphibians and reptiles exhibit different rates of growth and reach quite different sizes, both at maturity and at maximum size attained. Most animals increase in size as they age and the typical pattern is one of relatively rapid growth prior to the attainment of sexual maturity and then a decrease in the rate of growth or cessation of growth. Organisms that

Some changes take place during the late phases of development. In the Spiny hill tortoise *Geomyda spinosa* the serrations on the edge of the shell become reduced with increasing age.

attain a maximal size after which no change in size occurs are said to have determinate growth. Those which continue to increase in size, however slowly, over their entire lives are said to exhibit indeterminate growth. The trend among smaller species of amphibians and reptiles seems to be one of determinate growth, that of larger species of indeterminate growth. There is often a difference in the sizes of males and females of the same age as sexual maturity is approached and passed. American alligators are sexually mature at six years of age, for example, and at that age males are 6–7 ft (1·8–2·1 m) in length, the females 5–6 ft (1·6–1·8 m). Male alligators are usually larger than females of the same age, but among most amphibians and reptiles, it is the female that is larger. A detailed study of the Slider turtle *Pseudemys scripta* (Emydidae) in Panama revealed that male turtles had reached a plastron length of about $6\frac{1}{2}$ in (170 mm) at six years of age, whereas females averaged about $8\frac{1}{2}$ in (215 mm) at the same age. There is considerably more data available on growth rates of reptiles than for

amphibians, and much of the available information pertains to animals maintained in captivity. A galapagos turtle has been observed to gain 330 lb (150 kg) over seven years at an average rate of over 44 lb (20 kg) per year. Boa constrictors in captivity have been found to grow at a rate of almost 12 in (30 cm) a year until they reach a length of about 70 in (180 cm), after which growth slows. Relatively complete data for a captive Indian python *Python molurus molurus* (Boidae) over a 14 year period show that it grew at a rate of about 3 ft (0·9 m) per year until it reached a length of $9\frac{1}{2}$ ft (2·9 m) but only increased by 42 in (107 cm) over the next 12 years. Growth rate can be affected for amphibians and reptiles by extrinsic factors such as food availability or temperature, just as is larval development. The food factor makes rate determinations on captive specimens suspect because one never knows whether wild animals would have fed as often or as well as the captives. The effects of temperature can be seen in studies of species over different parts of their ranges, for example, in the Painted turtle *Chrysemys picta* (Emydidae) at four localities in the United States. At the northernmost locality in Wisconsin, males reached sexual maturity at a mean plastron length of 5 in (132 mm) at an age of 4 to 5 years. In Louisiana, at the southernmost study site, males reached sexual

Maximum adult size in snakes is achieved after a series of moults. The picture (left) shows the completely sloughed skin and the head of the Four-lined snake *Elaphe quatorlineata*. The adult form of some amphibians is extremely small; Corroboree toadlets *Pseudophrye corroboree* rarely exceed 1 in (2.5 cm) in length.

Ventral (bottom) view of a Tokay gecko *Gekko gecko*. The tail has been broken off and the newly-regenerated tip is clearly visible with a piece of shed skin adhering to it. Note also the lamellae under the toes which allow this lizard to climb smooth surfaces.

maturity at 2 to 3 years of age and at a plastron length of almost 3 in (73 mm) on the average.

Longevity. Data concerning the maximum longevity of amphibians and reptiles are based almost entirely on records of individuals in captivity. Again, these are suspect because captive animals do not face natural hazards such as inclement weather and predators and because they are often maintained under ideal environmental conditions with abundant food. Nevertheless, longevity is a subject of considerable interest and we discuss it here partly because there is much folk lore detailing the really fantastic age achieved by some animal or another, and much of this lore is incorrect.

Turtles, of course, hold the longevity records among amphibians and reptiles. Many species are known to live at least several decades and there is a confirmed record of a Giant tortoise *Testudo gigantea* (Testudinidae) from the Seychelles Islands of the Indian Ocean which lived for 152 years in captivity after being captured as an adult. Some crocodilians may rival the turtles in longevity, but the animal held longest in captivity was an American alligator which lived for 56 years. The Tuatara has

been known to live for at least 25 years and it is suspected that individuals might survive to over 100 years of age. This might be expected from the observations that Tuataras live 'slow' lives in a cool environment from a metabolic standpoint. The eggs incubate for more than a year, and sexual maturity is not reached until about 20 years of age. With some exceptions, lizards rarely live longer than 20 years and snakes 30 years in captivity for the longest-lived species. An exception is the European Slow worm *Anguis fragilis* (Anguidae) which survived 54 years. The Anaconda *Eunectes murinus* (Boidae) and a cobra *Naja melanoleuca* (Elapidae) have been kept for 29 years. The longevity record for amphibians seems to be held by a Giant asiatic salamander *Andrias japonicus* (Cryptobranchidae) which survived 55 years. A Boreal toad *Bufo boreas* (Bufonidae) lived 36 years, the longest known for a frog. Most long-lived frogs live less than 20 years, but several salamanders aside from *Andrias* have lived longer. The Greater siren *Siren lacertina* (Sirenidae), the Spotted salamander *Ambystoma maculatum* (Ambystomatidae) and the Japanese newt *Triturus pyrrhogaster* (Salamandridae) are all known to live

The Royal python *Python regius* is a relatively small snake, especially for its genus; this includes the reticulate python, *Python reticulatus*, one of the largest of snakes.

at least 25 years, and the Two-toed amphiuma *Amphiuma means* (Amphiumidae) has been found to survive for at least 27 years.

Size. There is much folk lore surrounding the subject of maximum sizes attained by various amphibians and reptiles, especially snakes. Qualified, unbiased recorders have rarely been present when truly large specimens have been encountered in nature and sometimes length estimates have been made from the skins of snakes and skulls of crocodilians. Snake skins are quite elastic and considerable stretching can occur if skins are prepared, and the precise relationships between skull length and total body length for crocodilians are only now being calculated. Restudy of earlier size estimates of supposedly record size crocodilians based on skull size almost always results in

'shrinkage'. Fewer individuals, usually specialists, are interested in minimum adult size, so fewer false assertions are probably made. The smallest living amphibian, as an adult, is the Cuban frog *Sminthillus limbatus* (Leptodactylidae) at less than $\frac{1}{2}$ in (12 mm). No salamanders are this short, but some of the lungless salamanders (Plethodontidae) at $1\frac{1}{2}$ in (40 mm) are very thin. The largest salamander by far is the Giant asiatic salamander *Andrias* which reaches a total length of 6 ft (180 cm). Others of the fully aquatic salamanders reach large sizes as well, much larger than any of the terrestrial species. The Two-toed amphiuma *Amphiuma means* has a recorded maximum total length of over 3 ft 9 in (116 cm), the Greater siren *Siren lacertina* almost 3 ft 2 in (98 cm), and the Hellbender *Cryptobranchus alleganiensis*, a North American relative of the Giant asiatic, 2 ft 5 in (74 cm). Among frogs, the record is held by the African giant frog *Conrana goliath* (Ranidae) with a recorded body length, excluding the outstretched hind limbs, of almost 1 ft (30 cm).

The smallest reptiles are lizards, with several species of the gecko *Sphaerodactylus* (Gekkonidae) measuring less than 2 in (5 cm) as adults. Some of the so-called microteids, such as *Bachia* (Teiidae) are also very small. The smallest snakes are species belonging to the families Typhlopidae and Leptotyphlopidae, the blind, burrowing snakes, which do not exceed 6 in (15 cm) in length. North American turtles of the genera *Kinosternon* and *Sternothaerus* (mud and musk turtles, respectively, family Kino-

The Yellow monitor *Varanus flavescens*, close relative of one of the largest lizards, the Komodo dragon *V. komodensis*, which attains a length of 9 ft (3 m).

The Rock plated lizard, a member of the genus *Gerrhosaurus*, members of which may exceed a length of 2 ft (60 cm).

sternidae), and the Bog turtle *Clemmys muhlenbergi* (Emydidae) all reach maximum sizes at about 4½ in (12 cm) and are the smallest turtles. And the smallest crocodilians are the Smooth-fronted caiman *Paleosuchus palpebrosus* (Alligatoridae) of South America at a maximum recorded size of 4 ft 9 in (145 cm), and the African dwarf crocodile *Osteolaemus osborni* (Crocodylidae) at just over 3 ft 9 in (114 cm).

As usual, it is the maxima that attract the attention, and the largest extant reptiles are truly large beasts. The largest turtle, without question, is the Leatherback turtle *Dermochelys coriacea* (Dermochelyidae) which may reach a weight of over

One of Europe's largest lizards, the Green lizard *Lacerta vividis*, 15 in (38 cm) in length.

1,500 lb (680 kg) and measure 6 ft (183 cm) in length (as measured over the curvature of the shell. The largest land turtles are the giant tortoises of the Seychelle Islands and Aldabra in the Indian Ocean, and the Galapagos Islands in the Pacific. The largest of these is a Galapagos tortoise *Testudo elephantopus* (Testudinidae) weighing about 560 lb (255 kg). There is also no question as to the largest lizard, which is the Komodo dragon *Varanus komodoensis* (Varanidae) from the Komodo Islands in the Indonesian Archipelago. This huge lizard reaches a length of at least 9 ft (3 m) and may weigh over 350 lb (160 kg). In the absence of other large carnivores on the island, the Komodo dragon has adopted the role preempted by tigers on other islands and is a scavenger of some note as well.

Controversy arises as we consider the giant crocodilians and snakes. Whereas there is often little argument as to the largest species, the sizes are often in question. The largest snakes, both belonging to the family Boidae, are the Reticulate python *Python reticulatus* of southeast Asia, and the Anaconda *Eunectes murinus* of South America. The best documented length for the former is 27 ft 6 in (8·4 m), for the latter 29 ft (9·1 m). Much greater lengths for both have been reported. The largest poisonous snake is the King cobra *Ophiophagus hannah* (Elapidae) which reaches almost 18 ft 4 in (5·6 m) in length. Four of the largest species of crocodilians are the American crocodile *Crocodylus acutus* and the Orinoco crocodile *C. intermedius* 23 ft (7 m) and the Nile crocodile *C. niloticus* 22 ft (6·7 m) all of which

63

belong to the family Crocodylidae; and the Indian gavial *Gavialis gangeticus* which is 21 ft 6 in (6·5 m) long and belongs to the family Gavialidae. All of these data for crocodilians are based on field measurements which are considered valid by most.

It should be apparent that many of the very large amphibians and reptiles are aquatic. This is easily explained. Water provides a great deal of support and permits large body size without disproportionately large supporting structures. It is thought that many of the large dinosaurs were semiaquatic for this reason. In fact, large aquatic amphibians and reptiles are often almost helpless on land because their appendages are designed for movement through water and not for support. All of the giant salamanders (*Siren, Amphiuma, Andrias, Cryptobranchus*) are aquatic and do poorly out of water although *Siren* and *Amphiuma*, having greatly reduced limbs, can move in a serpentine fashion. The giant sea turtles only return to land to lay their eggs, and the large snakes and crocodilians spend great amounts of time in water.

The Boa constrictor *Boa constrictor* is one of the snakes most commonly kept as pets. In nature, this snake may reach a length of about 18 ft (5.5 m).

Foods and Feeding

In this chapter, we will discuss eating. In later sections of this book, we will discuss being eaten. Detailed analyses of the feeding habits of most species of amphibians and reptiles are lacking, but we can get an idea on a broad scale of what most species eat. Like many other organisms, amphibians and reptiles exhibit food preferences, and what they are found to be eating at any given time may not really reflect what they will eat if more preferred foods are available or if their preferred foods are absent. Real problems arise in quantifying dietary information. Analysis of stomach contents is usually employed, but occasionally scats are examined or (for snakes) the animals are made to regurgitate.

Feeding Methods of Amphibians. Adult amphibians depend primarily on vision for locating and capturing food items. The major exception, of course, is afforded by the caecilians which are blind. These amphibians, however, have a tentacle which may be used to detect prey either by tactile or chemical stimulation. The sense of smell is rarely employed. Only animal food is eaten, and most species will take anything of proper size that is not noxious in taste or able to defend itself adequately, as by stinging. The food items actually eaten are determined by availability in the habitat of the amphibian, and by the method of feeding employed. There are major differences in the method of feeding of aquatic and terrestrial salamanders, and between the feeding methods of salamanders as a group and frogs. Aquatic salamanders employ what has been called the 'gape and suck' method of feeding. Many species of the family Salamandridae including representatives of the genera *Euproctus*, *Notophthalmus*, *Pleurodeles*, and *Taricha*, employ this method, as do hellbenders, mudpuppies and olms. The gape and suck method consists of the salamander approaching as close to the prey as possible, suddenly opening the mouth and expanding the throat. As water rushes into the mouth, the prey item is carried along with it and the mouth is rapidly shut over it. The tongues of salamanders utilizing this method of feeding are firmly attached to the floor of the mouth and cannot be pushed forward to any great extent. Terrestrial salamanders and the great majority of frogs, which are semiaquatic or terrestrial in habit, capture prey by rapidly projecting the tongue forward and out of the mouth or at least to the front margin of the mouth toward the prey. The tongue is equipped with a battery of mucous glands which render it somewhat sticky. The prey is ensnared on the surface of the tongue, which is then withdrawn into the mouth. This usually occurs so quickly that it is difficult to follow and the process has been studied using slow-motion photography. Tongue projection by salamanders may be accompanied by a lunge of the body toward the prey and this is observed among frogs too, but frogs have refined this technique to the point where a lunge is often unnecessary. This is because the tongue is often quite elastic and can be projected for some distance out of the mouth. In the American Bullfrog *Rana catesbeiana* (Ranidae), the tongue is arched forward toward the prey, contacting it before the arc is complete and wrapping around it: it is then quickly withdrawn, pulling the prey with it. The entire process takes less than 0·10 seconds! The fore limbs may be employed to help handle larger prey. The feeding behaviour of an aquatic anuran, the Clawed frog *Xenopus laevis*, is initiated as the potential prey item touches the outstretched fore limbs of the predator. The fore limbs are rapidly and repeatedly drawn toward the mouth, which is open, and the prey is simply grasped in the mouth and swallowed. The eyes of both salamanders and frogs can be withdrawn into the orbit, protruding into the mouth cavity to help force food into the oesophagus. Most amphibians have small teeth or none at all (for example, *Rhinophrynus* the Burrowing toad [Rhinophrynidae], and toads of the genus *Bufo* [Bufonidae]), but there are exceptions, as anyone who has ever been bitten by an even moderately large Congo eel *Amphiuma means* (Amphiumidae) can attest.

Larval salamanders feed in much the same manner as aquatic adults, but the mouth of a tadpole is drastically different from that of an adult frog and this is reflected both in the choice of foods and method of feeding. The methods of feeding employed by tadpoles are correlated with the habitat, more specifically the microhabitat, in which the tadpoles live. Tailed frog tadpoles are equipped with

White's treefrog *Hyla caerulea*, an Australian species, pulls its eye-balls back into their sockets to aid swallowing a mouse.

an oral disc which functions as a sucker to help hold them to rocks in the swift mountain streams in which they live. Within the disc, the mouth is provided with keratinized 'teeth' with which it scrapes algae off the rocks. There is little particulate matter available in the water column for them to exploit. Tadpoles inhabiting quieter waters, however, often exploit minute, unicellular plants and animals (phytoplankton and zooplankton) as well as other particulate matter in the water. Some tadpoles have the ability, through the use of a filtering mechanism, to capture suspended particles as small as 0.126μ (μ = micron; one micron = 1×10^{-6} m), a size comparable to that filtered out by the best mechanical sieves made by man. Water is taken in through the mouth, passes through the brachial apparatus before passing out through the spiracle or spiracles. The gill filters are able to remove larger particles, which then can move into the oesophagus, but smaller particles accumulate on branchial food traps which are equipped with a secretory ridge containing mucous glands. Clumps of cells and other matter form at the ridge until they are broken free by the flow of water and are moved toward the oesophagus. This system is most efficient in the Clawed frog *Xenopus laevis* (Pipidae) and *Rhinophrynus dorsalis* (Rhinophrynidae) which inhabit ponds rich in organic matter. The system is less efficient in the Grass frog *Rana pipiens* (Ranidae) which is a generalized tadpole, and least efficient in the Tailed frog

Ascaphus truei. As we have noted, Tailed frog tadpoles occur in fast-flowing water deficient in particulate matter. Pond tadpoles are often seen feeding in aggregations. The mass movements of the aggregation create whirlpools which concentrate particulate matter from the bottom of the pool so that it can be filtered by the mechanism outlined above.

Feeding Methods of Reptiles. The feeding habits and mechanisms of reptiles are considerably more diverse than those evidenced by the amphibians. This might be expected given the variation apparent in morphology as one compares, for example, turtles, snakes, and lizard-like reptiles. We will emphasize lizards and snakes in our discussion because of the variety of solutions to the problem of feeding these reptiles have evolved and because of the interesting problems associated with catching and subduing prey without the aid of limbs.

Turtles are omnivorous, eating both plant and animal matter. Most are scavengers as well. All living turtles lack teeth, although some extinct forms are known to have had them, but the jaw edges are sharp and sometimes jagged and covered with a horny material suitable for shearing. Although omnivores, turtles may have preferred food. Thus, the soft-shelled turtles *Trionyx* (Trionychidae) are primarily carnivorous, most pond turtles eat large amounts of plant material, and some musk turtles, like the Stripe-necked musk turtle *Sternothaerus peltifer* (Kinosternidae), favour snails. The sea turtles (Cheloniidae) and giant tortoises (Testudinidae) are primarily vegetarians. A few turtles have feeding specializations. One of the best known is the lure employed by the Alligator snapping turtle *Macrochelys temmincki* (Chelydridae). This turtle lies on the bottom of the rivers in which it lives with its mouth wide open to expose a worm-like lure on the floor of the mouth. The lure moves about and attracts the fish on which the turtle feeds. The Matamata *Chelys fimbricata* (Chelidae) uses a 'gape and suck' method. The turtle, like the Alligator snapper, is well camouflaged and lies in wait until a fish approaches. It then rapidly lowers the throat and thrusts the head forward with the mouth open. The prey is carried into the mouth as the water rushes in. This turtle also has a series of soft projections on the chin and neck which apparently detect water movements initiated by potential prey items (and other things). Most turtles probably rely a great deal on vision in detecting prey with the sense of smell

taking a secondary role. Crocodilians probably do the same. They either stalk large animal prey in the water, relying on slow movements and camouflage coupled with a rapid lunge at the end, or act as sit-and-wait predators until potential prey comes near enough for the lunge alone to bring results. It has been reported that they will use their powerful tail to subdue prey as well, and they will pull a large prey item into deep water, drowning it and dismembering it by rapidly rolling, thus twisting the prey.

Amphisbaenians are equipped with a rigid skull (unlike snakes) and sharp, curved, interlocking teeth. They also have well-developed temporal muscles. All of these allow them to both bite down effectively enough to crush bone or bite out pieces of flesh, and permit them to eat prey items larger than they are piece by piece. They are able to feed on earthworms and rodents with equal ease. Different feeding mechanisms are used by amphisbaenians depending upon whether potential prey is discovered at the surface or below ground. On the

A Snapping turtle, *Chelydra serpentina*. Although it lacks teeth, its jaws are covered with a sharp-edged horny 'beak'.

surface, the predator makes a short lunge and bites the prey. It then pulls the prey into its tunnel. The jaws are locked and pieces of the prey may be removed as the amphisbaenian withdraws into its tunnel, or as it twists its body. If prey is encountered in a tunnel, it is attacked as above or, if found alongside the body of the amphisbaenian, it is immobilized against the wall of the tunnel as the reptile moves backward until a sideward bite can be made. As a concession to limblessness, the amphisbaenian keeps the hind part of its body in the tunnel when it attacks prey above the surface, the tunnel providing an anchor.

Among lizards and snakes, vision and olfaction play important roles in prey location. Vision is of primary importance in lizards, many of which are attracted to prey by their movements, but some species are able to locate immobile prey, such as insect pupae, which are hidden from sight as well as quiescent. This is possible because they, along with snakes, have Jacobson's organs. These organs are found in all reptiles except adult crocodilians, but they are best developed in lizards and snakes. They are paired blind sacs lined with olfactory epithelium, innervated by the olfactory nerve, and located in the roof of the mouth. The tongues of lizards and snakes which use this form of olfaction are bifid (forked) and pick up airborne chemical cues on the tips. The tongue is then withdrawn into the mouth. The means by which particles at the tips of the tongue make their way into the Jacobson's organs is unknown with certainty. It was long assumed that the tips were inserted into the sacs, but in some lizards the duct leading into the organ is too small to admit even the tips of the tongue. It is possible that the tips are simply pressed against the openings of the ducts, but that still leaves the question of how particles enter the ducts and make their way to the olfactory epithelium in the sacs. The importance of the tongue (and Jacobson's organ) is without question. However, there still seems to be some disagreement as to the relative importance of the Jacobson's organ and the nasal apparatus.

Small lizards are primarily insectivorous and many larger lizards are carnivores, but the families Agamidae, Cordylidae, Iguanidae and Scincidae contain large species which are primarily herbivorous. Smaller members of these families are carnivorous, as are juvenile individuals of the larger members. It has been suggested that at least some large lizards are herbivorous for the following reasons. It takes a great deal of energy to chase and

catch a small insect and, when caught, the insect may not contain very much energy when compared to that spent catching it by a large lizard. Large lizards are less agile than smaller ones too, and each failure to catch an insect would result in a loss of energy in the chase that would have to be made up by subsequent captures. As the large lizard expends more energy each day than a smaller one, it seems more reasonable for it to concentrate on 'prey' that it can walk right up to with little cost in energy: plants. Plants are, of course, low in energy content,

The horny jaws of the Narrow-bridged mud turtle *Claudius angustatus* (opposite). Lack of teeth has not restricted the variety of foods taken by turtles. The Chameleon *Chamaelo dilepis* (below) catches prey with its incredibly long tongue.

The Gila monster *Heloderma suspectum*, although venomous, feeds mainly on defenseless small mammals and eggs.

crushing snail shells to get at the snail inside. Chameleons are the extreme specialists among lizards. They are superbly adapted to an arboreal existence. The family is characterized by a laterally flattened body, a prehensile tail, long limbs with quite flexible joints, hands and feet with digits arranged to oppose one another as the animal grasps the branch upon which it is standing with all four feet, the ability to change colours, and remarkable visual devices and tongue. The tongue is highly elastic and can be extended and retracted at great speed. At full extension, its length may exceed that of the body! The tip is thickened and supplied with mucous rendering it quite sticky. The eyes are on 'turrets', placed well away from the side of the head, and each turret can be moved in such a way that the animal can achieve binocular vision. The eyes also operate independently of one another, so that a chameleon can be looking at two things in different directions at the same time while assimilating all of this visual information without confusion in the brain. The method of prey capture employed is ambush. Any insect that comes within range of the tongue is picked off. The binocular vision affords the animal depth of field perception in this feat of marksmanship. So well adapted are chameleons to an arboreal existence that they are virtually helpless on the ground and probably descend only to lay eggs.

The final saurian specialization we will consider is exhibited by the only two members of the family Helodermatidae, the Gila monster *Heloderma suspectum* and the Beaded lizard *H. horridum*. These are, contrary to much popular opinion, the only poisonous lizards. Unlike poisonous snakes, to be discussed below, the venom glands of the lizards are located in the lower jaw. There is no connection between the venom gland and the teeth, all of which are grooved, but the venom is secreted into the mouth cavity and may travel down the grooves as the animal grasps its prey. *Heloderma* feeds primarily upon eggs (both of birds and reptiles) and small mammals and, although heavy-bodied, the Beaded lizard is at least partially arboreal.

Snakes exhibit three different means of prey capture: 'grab-and-swallow', constriction, and the use of poison to subdue their prey. There are obvious morphological adaptations associated with the latter two. The grab-and-swallow technique is employed by a wide variety of snakes, including many of the common, harmless species such as water snakes of the genus *Natrix* and garter snakes of the

so considerable material must be eaten, and it is difficult to digest compared with animal matter. For small, active lizards, this probably precludes an exclusively herbivorous habit. There are exceptions to this scheme of things. Some true chameleons (Chamaeleontidae) are large but are still insectivores, but the specialized means by which chameleons catch prey makes it economical to eat insects. Each capture requires very little energy, much less than a chase would involve. Some other small lizards are carnivorous at times, when insects are plentiful, and eat plant material at other times when insects are in short supply. *Ameiva exsul* (Teiidae) of Puerto Rico is one such lizard.

Specialized Feeding Methods. There are some feeding specializations exhibited by lizards. The Caiman lizard of South America *Dracaena guianensis* (Teiidae) is semiaquatic and snails form a major part of its diet. The teeth of this lizard, unlike those of other members of its family (and most other lizards), are broad and molar-like, an adaptation for

genus *Thamnophis* (both members of the family Colubridae). No special means of subduing the prey are employed and the teeth of such snakes are aglyphous, that is, solid and ungrooved. Like the teeth of all snakes, they are recurved. This facilitates feeding because, as the prey struggles in the mouth of the snake, it moves against the curve of the teeth in trying to move forward and out of the mouth. Its struggles, however, tend to move it backward, over the curved teeth and toward the oesophagus. Snakes using this feeding technique often swallow their prey alive.

Constrictors also have aglyphous teeth and these are often quite long, especially in those species which feed on birds. Many families are represented by constricting species. The most obvious is the Boidae, including all of the large constrictors like the pythons and Boa constrictor, but a number of colubrid genera, for example the Rat snakes *Elaphe*, and the king snakes *Lampropeltis*, constrict as do members of certain other families. The African snake, Bibron's burrowing viper *Atractaspis bibronii*, which may belong to the family Viperidae, also constricts. Constrictors strike at their prey and subdue it by wrapping coils of the body around it. The prey is not crushed, but suffocated for, every time it exhales, the snake tightens the coils until the prey can no longer expand its lungs. After a time, the snake relaxes and begins to swallow the prey. There are several thoughts on how the snake determines

The Tentacled snake *Erpeton tentaculatum* feeds almost exclusively on fish.

This king snake *Lampropeltis* is constricting a mouse. The prey dies of suffocation and is not crushed.

that the prey is indeed dead. These include cessation of respiratory movements and detection of the heart beat, among others. Both constrictors and venomous snakes generally swallow the prey head first so that the legs fold back naturally and the snake does not have to swallow around them. This behaviour is apparently learned in some species whose young will often try to swallow prey tail first or even sideways but experienced snakes rarely do. Conversely, studies of newborn Rat snakes *Elaphe obsoleta* (Colubridae) show that they swallow prey head first, so this behaviour may be innate (inherited) in this and possibly some other species. King cobras *Ophiophagus hannah* (Elapidae) and Coral snakes *Micrurus fulvius* (Elapidae) use the direction of scale overlap of the snakes they eat as the cue to locate the head for head first swallowing. Although the predator may grab a snake at midbody, it unerringly moves its grasp toward the head. If the skins on dead snakes are reversed and fed to Coral snakes and cobras, the predators move their grasp toward the tail. Constrictors kept in captivity learn to eat food that is dead when they

Swallowing prey tail-first is difficult, as this Australian tiger snake *Notechis scutatus* is discovering. Note the opaque eye of this individual, which will soon shed its skin.

After the prey is dead, constrictors like this Royal python *Python regius* move it in order to swallow it head-first.

Like all pit vipers, this Crossed viper *Bothrops alternatus* (above) has a heat-sensing pit on each side of the head to aid its strike and help track prey. The tentacles on the head of the Fishing snake *Herpeton tentaculatum* (right) are also thought to help sense the presence of prey.

receive it, and often omit constriction all together, simply taking the food in the mouth and swallowing it.

Venomous Snakes. The most advanced prey capture method is employed by the venomous snakes of the families Colubridae, Viperidae and Elapidae. All possess a venom gland and fangs. The fangs of poisonous colubrids, such as the Lyre snake *Trimorphodon lambda* and the Boomslang *Dispholidus typus*, are not hollow but grooved. They are termed opisthoglyphous and are located at the rear of the mouth. Thus, these snakes are commonly called rear-fanged snakes. The venom of most is not lethal to man, although many can cause discomfort, and some, including the Boomslang, have caused death to humans. Venom is introduced into the prey as the snake chews after striking and, although the fangs are at the rear of the mouth, humans who have been bitten by rear-fanged snakes attest to the rapidity with which the fangs are brought into play. The elapid snakes, including the cobras, sea snakes and coral snakes, have proteroglyphous fangs. These are relatively short, hollow or deeply grooved (effectively hollow) fangs firmly fixed to the maxillary bone at the front of the upper jaw. The venom gland is connected to the hollow fang by a duct. As

the snake strikes, muscles surrounding the venom gland contract and venom is injected much as a hypodermic syringe injects. Many of the elapid snakes are extremely venomous and dangerous to man. The final group of poisonous snakes is the family Viperidae, including the Old and New World vipers and the New World rattlesnakes, copperheads and water moccasins. These snakes, many of which are lethal to man, have an advanced venom delivery apparatus involving relatively large, hollow fangs situated on a movable maxilla so that they can be folded back against the sides of the jaw. As the snake strikes, the mouth is opened wide and the fangs erected so that they stab into the prey. Venom is rapidly injected as the muscles around the venom gland contract. Because the action is a stabbing one and the fangs are long, any size prey (or enemy) may

73

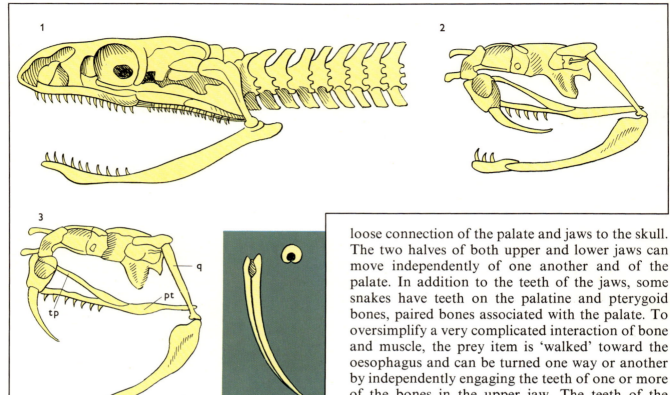

Cranial anatomy of snakes. (1) Skull of a generalized snake in side view. (2) A Rattlesnake skull, showing the elongate fangs in the upper jaw. When the jaws open (3) these fangs rotate forwards on the hinged quadrate (q), pterygoid (pt) and transpalatine (tp) bones. The fang has a poison gland in its base (inset).

be attacked. The action of the venom may be reasonably slow, and viperids often have to track their prey to where it has died after the strike. The means by which this is done will be discussed later. Elapids must bite down on their prey to inject venom, and this restricts somewhat the size of prey taken, but the action of the venom may be extremely rapid. The so-called spitting cobras, such as the African spitting cobra *Naja nigricollis*, are able to eject venom forcefully and with great accuracy at potential enemies, often aiming directly at the eyes.

Most snakes can swallow prey larger around than they are. This is most apparent in the constrictors, but it is not restricted to them. Several things make it possible. The skin of snakes is very elastic and can stretch around a large prey item as it is swallowed. The two halves of the lower jaw are joined at the front end by a ligament and not rigidly fused, allowing them to spread apart. There is, especially in so-called advanced snakes such as viperids, a very

loose connection of the palate and jaws to the skull. The two halves of both upper and lower jaws can move independently of one another and of the palate. In addition to the teeth of the jaws, some snakes have teeth on the palatine and pterygoid bones, paired bones associated with the palate. To oversimplify a very complicated interaction of bone and muscle, the prey item is 'walked' toward the oesophagus and can be turned one way or another by independently engaging the teeth of one or more of the bones in the upper jaw. The teeth of the pterygoid can be engaged on one side and moved backwards, pulling the prey along, as the pterygoid on the other side moves forward. Of course, in handling a prey item, teeth may be broken, but these are replaced. Examination of a snake skull will reveal new teeth developing beneath functional ones and replacement, even of the fangs in solenoglyphs, is normal. Tooth replacement occurs among lizards as well and the beginnings of the independent movement of the upper jaw on the braincase are seen there too. The skulls of many lizards (for example, *Varanus*, Varanidae) are movable at several points.

All snakes are carnivorous. Small snakes may eat insects, earthworms or other invertebrates whereas larger snakes prey upon small birds, mammals or small reptiles and amphibians. Very large snakes are primarily predators of birds and mammals and this is true of viperids of all sizes. Some snakes have specialized diets and morphological adaptations for them. Schlegel's viper *Bothrops schlegelii* (Viperidae) is arboreal and equipped with a prehensile tail. It is reputed to lie in wait along paths and other avian flyways in Middle American forests, ambush-

Four of the stages by which an egg-eating snake of the ▷ genus *Dasypeltis* swallows its food. Note the tremendous elasticity of the skin, such that the scales are spread well apart. The vertical pupil of the eye indicates that the snake is active at night.

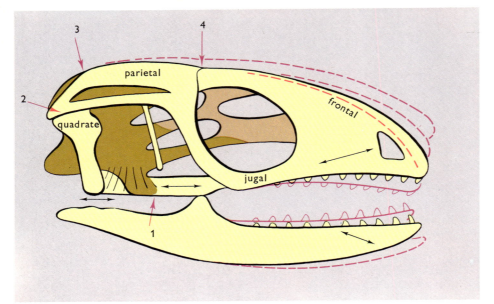

Diagram showing the possible range of movements and movable joints in kinesis of lizards. The occipital region (dark parts) is 'fixed' through its attachment to the rest of the body. The bones of the skull are variously movable on the joints (1–4) allowing the lizard to both raise the upper jaw and lower the lower jaw to swallow larger prey.

The long, flexible tongue of the Komodo dragon *Varanus komodoensis* with which it senses the air and substrate around it. In spite of many similarities with snakes, the Komodo dragon is not venomous.

ing birds, sometimes in flight! Several snake species are adapted for egg eating. Members of the genera *Dasypeltis* and *Elachistodon* (Colubridae) are best known for this. The ventral projections (hypapophyses) of the cervical (neck) vertebrae are elongate and extend into the oesophagus and the skin of the mouth, the cheek is extremely elastic and the teeth are small and reduced in number. As an egg is swallowed whole, it encounters the cervical hypapophyses and is broken. The contents of the egg are swallowed and the broken shell regurgitated. Two other genera of colubrid snakes, *Aplopeltura* and *Pareas*, are specialist feeders of snails and slugs. The shell of a snail is not crushed. The snake uses its teeth to slowly pull the snail out of its shell. The two halves of the lower jaw in these snakes cannot be widely spread as in most snakes.

Other Venomous Reptiles. Finally, some additional comments concerning venoms are in order. Reptilian venoms are chemically quite complex and it is not possible, as is often done in popular literature, to divide venomous reptiles according to whether the action of the venom is on the nervous system (neurotoxic) or on the blood cells and blood vessels (haemolytic). Snake venoms contain both neurotoxic and haemolytic components, although one or other may predominate. Thus for elapids there is very little tissue damage at the site of the wound following the bite of most species and the primary effects are paralysis and respiratory difficulties. Viperid venoms have obvious haemolytic properties and result in haemorrhage at the site of the strike and destruction of red blood cells, the

lining of the blood vessels and a reduction in the ability of the blood to coagulate ('clot'). *Heloderma* venom is considered primarily neurotoxic in nature. Not all venomous snakes, as mentioned above, are lethal to man. Even many of the elapids, for example, possess venom which has no drastic effect. Some snakes are immune to their own venom in normal doses. The extremely venomous Australian tiger snake *Notechis scutatus* (Elapidae) required a dose of its own venom that was relatively 180,000 times greater than that required to kill a guinea pig before it succumbed. King snakes *Lampropeltis* (Colubridae) are ophiophagus; that is, they eat snakes, and they do not hesitate to attack a rattlesnake. In fact, rattlesnakes exhibit a specific defence behaviour when confronted by a king snake or even the odour of a king snake, and king snakes are immune to the effects of rattlesnake venom. Venomous snakes are capable of administering varying doses of venom, apparently in response to prey size, and venomous snakes are venomous at any age. A new-born rattlesnake is quite venomous, although it may not be able to deliver a very large dose. There is evidence that snake venoms differ from place to place within the range of a species, and that their exact composition is adjusted to cope with the type of prey encountered. Changes in venom composition also occur as a snake ages, and these might reflect changes in prey species utilized by the snake. In some parts of the world, notably the Indian subcontinent, snake bite is still a major source of human mortality. We will discuss this further in the last chapter of this book.

By now it should be apparent that amphibians and reptiles are truly diverse both ecologically and morphologically. To a great extent, the latter diversity is a result of the former, with special morphological adaptations evolving among amphibians and reptiles occupying certain habitats. Amphibians and reptiles are also extremely diverse in their methods of movement, which are again correlated with the morphologies of the organisms and ultimately their ecologies. Both amphibians and reptiles run the gamut from completely limbless forms to fully tetrapod species, and are represented by species that walk, run, jump, swim, climb and even 'fly'. In this chapter, we will see how amphibians and reptiles move.

Swimming on Land. The locomotion of salamanders is probably most primitive, for it is most similar to that employed by fishes. Aquatic salamanders, even those with well-developed limbs, move by lateral undulations of the body if they are moving through the water and not crawling along the bottom. The curves of the body thrust against the resistance offered by the water and propel the animal forward. Although the entire body undulates, the laterally flattened or keeled tail increases the effective surface area of the animal, giving maximum 'push' against the water. In aquatic

salamanders that have reasonably well-developed limbs, these are folded back against the sides when the animal is swimming. Essentially the same type of locomotion is observed among terrestrial salamanders even though the limbs are brought into play. The limbs of salamanders are lateral in position and do not substantially lift the body as do the more ventrally positioned legs of birds and mammals, so the body more or less sprawls and cannot be lifted far off the ground. The body is still thrown into a curve as the animal moves forward with first the left front and right rear feet contacting the ground as the right front and left rear feet are brought forward, then the right front and left rear feet provide the push as the left front and right rear feet move forward. When viewed from above, the body is seen to undulate in a manner similar to that of a swimming fish. On land, this is not a very efficient means of locomotion, energy being wasted just keeping the body off the ground as it is not supported from beneath to any great extent.

Jumping. Frogs are specialized for hopping or jumping even though some species really walk rather than do either. The toad *Atelopus ignescens* (Bufonidae) of the Andes in South America has relatively short legs and moves along slowly, even if approached quite closely, by walking. The generalized

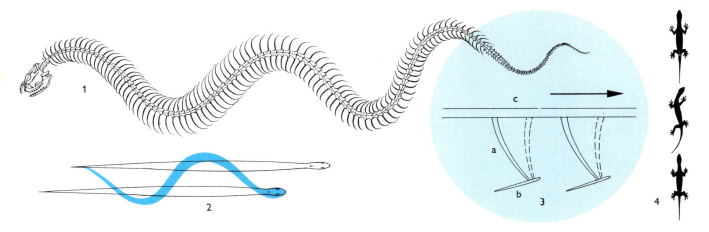

European tree frogs *Hyla arborea* (left). Note the expanded tips of the toes which enable these frogs to climb with great agility.

(1) Snakes may have up to 200 pairs of ribs, attached to scales on the underside of the body. (2) In locomotion the snake grips the ground with the underside of the head; it then twists its body, lowers its tail to the ground and stretches itself out. (3) Many snakes use the ribs (a) for slow movements, levering the scales (b) against the backbone (c). (4) Lizards walk with sinuous body movements reminiscent of those of fish.

A striking picture of the North American green frog _Rana clamitans_ leaping.

frog skeleton is highly modified in some respects for saltation (jumping). The number of vertebrae between the limb girdles (presaeral vertebrae) are reduced to eight (in the Leiopelmatidae) or nine, and the tail (caudal) vertebrae are fused into a rodlike bone called a urostyle, the combination providing the rigidity necessary for jumping. In addition, the hind limbs of frogs are often quite long and well-muscled. The fore limbs, which do not provide propulsion for a jump, function to support the front part of the frog when resting, much as the nose wheel of an aeroplane does, and to absorb the shock of landing. The fore limbs are useful on occasion to dislodge an irritant from the head or around the mouth and the hands are very important in walking and climbing. The hind feet of semiaquatic and aquatic frogs are webbed and push against the resistance of the water as the frog swims in the familiar 'frog kick' manner. Some of the large tree frogs of South America (for example, _Hyla miliaris_, Hylidae) and southeast Asia (for example, _Rhacophorus nigropalmatus_, Ranidae) have large webs between the digits of both the hands and feet. They are capable of leaping from a tree and gliding for long distances over a slanting path, thus escaping potential predators and earning themselves the name 'flying frogs' even though true flight is not involved. A few studies have been carried out relating the distance a frog can jump to characteristics of the frog. It has been discovered that, in the giant tropical toad _Bufo marinus_ (Bufonidae) from Brazil, a toad twice as long (measured from the snout tip to the tip of the urostyle) as another, weighed eight times as much, had hind legs twice as long, and could jump twice as far.

Aquatic caecilians swim by laterally undulating the body as described for salamanders, and they may retain some of the larval fin as adults or the hind part of the body may be laterally compressed. In their burrows, caecilians move by a form of concertina locomotion (described more fully for snakes below) whereby the body is shortened by multiple curves in the vertebral column _within_ the body. The curvature slightly widens the body at one particular point so that it presses against the walls of the burrow and the head and body ahead of the fixed point are moved forward. Then a more forward point can be fixed against the walls of the burrow and the rear of the animal moved up. Actually, many points are fixed at the same time, with forward movement going on simultaneously in several sections of the animal's body. The skin of caecilians contains numerous mucous glands, and the mucous produced lubricates the skin and reduces friction.

The limbs of this Hawksbill turtle *Eretmochelys imbricata* are admirably shaped for the flight type of locomotion these turtles employ in the water. The shell of this turtle was once prized for commercial uses but plastics have largely replaced it. Note the Remora fish about to attach itself to the plastron of the turtle, where it will feed on material dropped by its host.

Turtles, by virtue of their encasement in a usually rigid shell, are entirely dependent on their limbs for locomotion. There are three recognizable types of limbs. The land turtles, such as the Galapagos tortoise *Testudo elephantopus* (Testudinidae) have pillar-like legs reminiscent of those of an elephant. The toes are short and unwebbed. Aquatic and semiaquatic turtles other than the sea turtles have less robust limbs and feet and there is a 'heel'. There may be a good deal of webbing between the toes of the hind feet or of both the hind and front feet. Webbing is especially prominent on the feet of the highly aquatic soft-shelled turtles (*Trionyx*, Trionychidae). Some of the smaller land turtles in the family Testudinidae and such other primarily terrestrial species like the box turtles, *Terrapene* (Emydidae) have a foot-type intermediate to the two just described. Finally, sea turtles are the most aquatic of the turtles. Once they make their way to the water after hatching, males may never return to the land and females only to lay eggs. The only known exceptions are Green sea turtles *Chelonia mydas* (Cheloniidae) which come ashore to bask in some parts of the world. The limbs of sea turtles (Cheloniidae and Dermochelyidae) are paddle-like, the fore limbs more so than the hind limbs. They are fast and graceful swimmers, moving their fore limbs, which provide propulsion, in a manner suggesting flight. The hind limbs aid in steering. One freshwater turtle, the New Guinea soft-shelled turtle *Carettochelys insculptata* (Carettochelyidae) has paddle-like fore limbs. These are the only turtles whose fore limbs provide most of the propulsion; in other turtles this function is that of the hind limbs. On land, large sea turtles move with difficulty, hitching

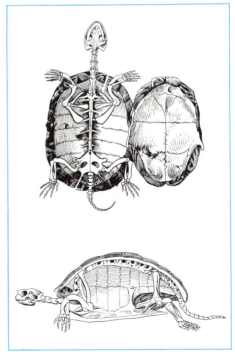

Skeleton of a turtle. (Top) With the plastron separated and laid to one side the skeleton is exposed, showing backbone, pectoral and pelvic girdles and limbs. (Bottom) Longitudinal section showing integration of backbone with carapace.

81

The paddle-like limbs of sea turtles are virtually useless on land. This female Leatherback turtle *Dermochelys coriacea* is slowly returning to the sea after laying her eggs on the beach.

themselves forward by synchronous movement of all four limbs. Baby sea turtles, moving from nest to sea, scuttle along using the limbs in the normal way, the paddles moving alternately.

Crocodilians have the ability to pull the limbs in toward the body, the effect being to raise the body off the ground. They can then accomplish what has been termed a 'high walk'. The gait is a diagonal walk, the diagonal feet (that is, front left and hind right) touching the ground at about the same time and diagonal legs moving synchronously or nearly so. As a crocodilian does this, its archosaurian descent is betrayed by the fact that the hind legs are longer than the fore legs causing the body to slope downwards from the hip. This high walk is used when crocodilians are away from the water. They can also crawl slowly or move very rapidly with the legs sprawled apart, the belly on the ground, perhaps the most common form of terrestrial locomotion. In 1961 Cott reported for the first time that crocodilians can gallop. He observed small Nile crocodiles *Crocodylus niloticus* (Crocodylidae) galloping at an estimated 6·8–8 mph (11–13 kph). In doing so, the

fore limbs and hind limbs work as pairs. As the fore limbs push backward on the ground, the hind limbs are brought forward. Then the hind limbs push off against the ground as the fore limbs are stretched forward. This gait is apparently rarely used. Crocodilians have also been reported to run bipedally, with the fore limbs held off the ground, but this too must be rare. When swimming, the limbs are held against the sides and propulsion is provided by the powerful, keeled tail.

Lizard Locomotion. Lizards show the greatest diversity of methods of locomotion, and only partially because an entire spectrum of limb development from no limbs at all to the full tetrapod condition is realized. A so-called 'typical' lizard might be exemplified by the Sand lizard *Lacerta agilis* (Lacertidae). If a child were asked to draw the outline of an 'ordinary' lizard, the outline might well fit the Sand lizard. The body is of moderate proportions, the limbs well developed and equipped with five toes, and the tail is slender and longer than

The Chameleon *Chamaeleo dilepis* has opposable toes that enable it to grasp branches while climbing.

the body. The Sand lizard is active primarily on the ground, but it can burrow and climb steep banks and rock faces with ease. When this lizard moves, it does so in a typical tetrapod fashion, employing all four limbs whether walking along slowly in search of food or running from the threat of an enemy. Although it can swim, it does so only if chased into the water or finds itself there by accident. It does not normally climb into vegetation.

Many lizards with no more specializations than described for the Sand lizard are adept climbers and can be classified ecologically as arboreal or saxicolous (rock dwelling). Such a lizard is the Desert spiny lizard *Sceloporus magister* (Iguanidae) which is primarily arboreal in many areas but saxicolous or terrestrial to a greater or lesser extent in other areas. The lizard has well developed limbs and feet

evidenced by some of the geckos and by anoles involve the feet as well. These lizards are famous for their ability to run up apparently smooth walls and across vertical glass surfaces, and some of the geckos can actually move upside-down across a ceiling to catch insects near a light. Some of this climbing ability can be attributed to sharp, recurved claws, but not all of it. In the first place, such claws would be of little use on extremely smooth surfaces and, secondly, some very good climbing geckos do not have such claws. The claws are essential on rough surfaces, however. On smooth surfaces, both geckos and anoles depend upon the wide scales under each toe, the subdigital lamellae. These lamellae are absent from the toes of non-climbing geckos such as the Little yellow-headed gecko *Gonatodes fuscus* or the Banded gecko *Coleonyx variegatus*. Only a few

A gecko using its tongue as a windscreen wiper to clean the surface of its eye (left). The underside of the front foot of a Climbing gecko, showing the enlarged subdigital lamellae (scales) which enable it to grip while climbing (right).

equipped with sturdy claws but, other than that, has no special morphological adaptations for climbing. The most specialized climbing lizards are the true chameleons (Chamaeleontidae), certain of the geckos (for example, the Tokay gecko *Gekko gecko*) and the anoles, *Anolis* (Iguanidae). The toes of chameleons are arranged in two groups opposing one another on the feet in the same sense that your thumb opposes the rest of your fingers. On the front feet, there are three toes on the inside, two on the outside; this is reversed on the hind feet. The toes of a group are united throughout their lengths except for the last joint and the claws. A chameleon can move along a narrow branch by clasping it with the feet and moving one forward at a time, very, very slowly. An additional point of contact with the branch is afforded by the highly prehensile tail. The primary adaptations for an arboreal existence

iguanid genera other than *Anolis* have such expanded lamellae, and all climb as does *Anolis*. The tremendous climbing ability of these lizards is attributed to the exceedingly fine setae found on each lamella. These hair-like structures are only about four thousandths of an inch (0·1 mm) in length, but each branches repeatedly so that there are from 100 to 1,000 'branch tips'. Each of these tips is a microscopic suction cup. Each foot has hundreds of thousands of these multi-branched setae. The tiny suction cups allow the lizards to adhere to smooth, dry surfaces. Only the use of electron microscopy permitted these structures to be seen and the phenomenal climbing abilities of these lizards to be explained.

One of the climbing geckos, the Malayan bent-toed gecko *Cyrtodactylus pulchellus*, belongs to a group of geckos which lack expanded subdigital lamellae and setae. The toes of this gecko are bent such that the claws are at right angles to the climbing surface and, although not as adept as the Tokay gecko and its allies, it is able to climb rough surfaces with ease.

Many of the arboreal lizards, including *Anolis* but not the geckos, also have long, relatively narrow tails. For these fast-moving species, the tail serves as a balancer as the lizard moves along narrow branches.

The forests of southeast Asia harbour the only 'flying' lizards, and these, like the flying frogs, really glide rather than fly. Lizards of the genus *Draco* (Agamidae) have the most spectacular morphological innovation for flight. These lizards do not look unlike an anole as they sit on a tree trunk or branch, but when molested, the animal unfolds a pair of 'wings' along its sides and jumps. Glides exceeding 20 ft (6 m) have been observed. The wings are really flaps of skin supported internally by several elongate ribs which can be folded back against the sides of the lizard when not in use. The glide is downward for the most part, but turns up just before the lizard alights on a tree trunk or branch. The skin of the wings is brightly coloured and also functions in courtship. There are gliding geckos as well, exemplified by the Parachute gecko *Ptychozoon kuhli*. The toes of these lizards are webbed, and there is a loose fold of skin along the sides between the legs and on the tail. These cannot be spread in the same manner as the wings of *Draco*, but are opened as the lizard extends its legs and tail, and spreads its toes. The parachute geckos, unlike *Draco*, fall more or less directly downward but remain upright and land unhurt. Some other lizards, including *Anolis*, assume the same posture as the parachute geckos when dropped and have weak parachuting capabilities. Unlike non-parachuting lizards, they do not turn and twist in panic as they fall.

Getting back to the ground, we find some lizards which are able to run bipedally, on just the hind legs. A number of lizards in the families Agamidae and Iguanidae are noted for this. All have the hind legs longer than the front legs, and all have long, balancing tails, the same morphological adaptations seen in kangaroos and some of the long extinct dinosaurs. In fact, the Collared lizard *Crotaphytus collaris* (Iguanidae) resembles a small version of *Tyrannosaurus rex*! These lizards achieve bipedal stance only at high speeds and often run this way to escape from predators. The Basilisk lizard *Basiliscus* (Iguanidae) of South and Central America is often found in trees, but can run rapidly and bipedally. It is noted for its ability to run some distance over the surface of water, being supported by surface tension. The toes of the hind legs are very long and are spread wide as the lizard hits the water at high speed, so the animal's weight is distributed over a wide area. The lizard is locally known as the 'Jesus Cristo lagarto' (Jesus Christ lizard) because of this ability.

Some of the lizards found in sandy habitats have evolved special adaptations for movement over or through sand. Some of these will be discussed when we consider burrowing adaptations below. Several lizards have the ability to 'sand swim'. These lizards, exemplified by the fringe-toed lizards, *Uma* (Iguanidae), Cantor's fringe-toed lizard *Acanthodactylus cantoris* (Lacertidae), and the Sandfish *Scincus philbyi* (Scincidae), all have a fringe of scales on the toes. These help support the animal on loose, fine sand and allow it to 'swim' beneath the surface. If a *Uma* is chased, it usually runs just out of sight, behind a small bush for example, or over a dune, and then dives into the sand. The head is wedge-shaped, allowing easy entry. Under the sand, the fringes on the toes fold as the limbs are drawn forward, but stand out as the limbs are pushed back. The added surface area facilitates movement through the sand, and if the lizard is to be caught, one must dig some distance in front of its point of entry into the sand.

Limbless Reptiles. Limb reduction or loss has occurred in several lizard families. The families Pygopodidae, Dibamidae, Anelytropsidae, Cordylidae, Scincidae, Teiidae, Anguidae and Annillidae have some form of reduction. Sometimes, as in the Anelytropsidae and Anniellidae, the entire group is completely limbless. In others, the limbs are reduced to flaps: Dibamidae (females are limbless, males have flap-like hind limbs only) and Pygopodidae. The other families have both fully tetrapod species and species with some degree of limb reduction or outright loss. The skinks are a prime example of the latter. The large Australian Shingleback skink *Trachydosaurus rugosus* has well-developed limbs, whereas the Cylindrical skink *Chalcides chalcides* from North Africa has tiny limbs. A similar range is evident among the Philippine short-legged skinks *Brachymeles* and skinks of the genus *Scelotes* in Africa and Madagascar. Even if there has been complete loss of the limbs, the pelvic and pectoral girdles remain.

Limbless lizards can be divided into two groups: those which are active primarily on the surface (for

During the evolution of the lizards, limbs have frequently been reduced to produce snake-like forms such as this Galliwasp *Diploglossus tenuifasciatus*.

example, the Slow worm *Anguis fragilis*, Anguidae) and the burrowers. The latter can be further categorized as to habitat: sand-dwellers (for example, the Cylindrical skink) and those found in areas where leaf litter accumulates (for example, the microteid *Bachia*). At the surface, lizards which have no limbs or considerable limb reduction move in a serpentine fashion by lateral undulation. Only when moving slowly are much reduced limbs used. Burrowing is accomplished with the head, which is pushed through the soil or litter. The head scales of these lizards are often reduced in number through fusion one with another or are arranged in such a fashion that they add rigidity to the skull.

Finally, in our discussion of lizards, some mention must be made of aquatic species. Some of the extinct lizards were fully aquatic, but living lizards are at most semiaquatic. The best known of these is the Galapagos marine iguana *Amblyrhynchus cristatus* (Iguanidae). In this species, the feet are slightly webbed and the tail compressed. The tail is the means of propulsion in the water, the feet functioning to steer but are normally folded alongside the body. Many primarily terrestrial species occasionally enter the water, even the desert-dwelling Gila monster *Heloderma suspectum* can swim, but none have special adaptations for swimming.

All amphisbaenians are burrowers, and all but

Bipes (Bipedidae) are limbless. *Bipes* retains tiny fore limbs which resemble hands stuck onto the body. Carl Gans has contributed extensively to the study of locomotion in these and other 'limbless tetrapods'. He recognizes four head shapes among amphisbaenians: round, spade-shaped, vertically keeled, and wedge-shaped with lateral edges. Each begins a burrow by driving the head into the ground. The skull in these reptiles is very solid and the scales are arranged for added support. Once the tunnel is begun, each of the four types of amphisbaenians as identified by head shape extend the tunnel by different methods. The simplest method is employed by the round-headed species (for example, *Amphisbaena darwini*, Amphisbaenidae; *Bipes biporus*, Bipedidae) which ram the head into the soil, compacting it by pushing it aside. The small fore limbs of *Bipes* are used to scratch a cavity as a tunnel is begun at the surface. The spade-snouted species (for example, *Rhineura floridana*, Amphisbaenidae) drive the snout forward into the bottom of the tunnel, then lift the snout compacting the soil and widening the tunnel before the next penetrating thrust. Keel-headed amphisbaenians (for example, *Mesobaena anchietae*, Amphisbaenidae) use a variant of the two-cycle (ram and widen) used by the spade-snouted species. The keel-snouted species drive the snout into the middle of the face of the tunnel, then compact and widen by moving the head from side to side. Finally, members of the family Trogonophidae, such as *Agamodon anguliceps*, burrow by oscillating the head first one direction, then the other, peeling off thin layers of soil with the edges of the wedge-shaped snout and compacting it against the sides of the burrow with the sides of the head. Members of this latter family have bodies shaped like an inverted U with the opening closed over, or they are laterally compressed. If they were cylindrical, as are other amphisbaenians, they would tend to turn on their long axis in the tunnel as the head oscillates and, with no bracing, the animal would have difficulty in extending the tunnel. In the burrow, amphisbaenians can move forward or backward with equal facility using rectilinear and concertina methods of locomotion. These will be described as we consider snakes.

Snakes. Snakes have been severely restricted in their modes of locomotion by virtue of their limblessness, as have the other limbless amphibians and reptiles we have considered. But snakes have been extremely successful without limbs, as evidenced by the range of habitats they occupy and by

The Slow worm *Anguis fragilis* has no externally visible limbs although it is a lizard and not a snake.

the number of species. Four basic modes are recognized, two of which have already been at least mentioned in our discussion of caecilian, lizard and amphisbaenian locomotion: lateral undulation, concertina, rectilinear and side-winding. Many snakes can use any of these modes, but some are used more often than others, and some are used in particular environments and rarely in others. Whichever means of locomotion is employed, it is dependent upon contact between the snake and the substrate. The usual point of contact is the lower surface of the snake which is covered with wide scales with trailing edges that overlap the front portion of the scale behind. Generally, each of these ventral scales is associated with a single row of scales

on the sides and body, and with a single vertebra and the single set of muscles. We will see how these anatomical features interact as snakes use each of the four basic modes of locomotion.

Lateral undulation is the most common means of locomotion and is adopted by some lizards which have limbs, these being folded back along the body, as well as by all other limbless tetrapods. It is used on the ground and by arboreal forms moving horizontally through vegetation. When a snake or any other limbless tetrapod uses lateral undulation, the propelling force is not directed downward against the ground, but laterally against irregularities such as fixed pebbles or tufts of grass. A wavelike muscular contraction moves down the animal's

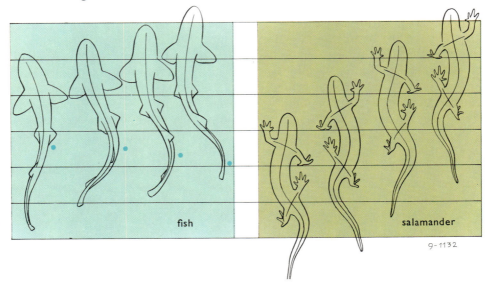

In fish, the body is thrown into curves passing down the body and providing thrust. In a salamander, the body is thrown into curves, but the swing of the front and hind limbs and the alternate lifting of right and left limbs carry the body forward.

fish

salamander

9-1132

The hind part of the body of this snake *Liasis child-reni* shows clearly how it is thrown into lateral undulations.

body, the loop so formed remaining against the irregularity but moving backwards on the body of the snake. Several loops are employed, each exerting a force on a different irregularity. As the snake moves forward, new irregularities are encountered and new loops form. At least three contact points must be maintained for forward movement to occur, two of these can be on one side, but the third must be on the other to prevent sideways movement instead of forward movement. Lateral undulations are not possible on a smooth, flat surface, nor in a tunnel for pressure cannot be exerted against the sides. Rectilinear locomotion is better under these circumstances, but it requires a certain combination of muscles and bone structure unavailable to most snakes.

Rectilinear locomotion is more efficient than lateral undulation for large, heavy bodied snakes and is used by, for example, the boas and pythons. Movement is accomplished as the snake fixes to the ground a series of ventral scales that lie near the head; it then moves its head forwards. As the skin stretches out, the forward-most fixed scales are lifted out of contact with the ground, but scales to the rear are pulled up to join the fixed series. Two or three zones are fixed to the ground along the length of the snake and these move continuously to the rear as the snake moves forward, whilst new fixed zones are established near the head. The two sides of the snake move together and a snake may move forward while maintaining the body in nearly a straight line. Of course, a very loose association between the skin and underlying muscles is essential for rectilinear locomotion. The propelling force is exerted downward and to the rear, rather than laterally as in lateral undulation, and friction between the lower surface of the snake and the ground is important.

Concertina locomotion is used by snakes which lack the anatomical requirements for rectilinear movement. When moving in this fashion, the snake

The Eastern green mamba *Den-droaspis angusticeps* is a much feared venomous snake of Africa; it is also an accomplished climber, as evidenced by its long, thin body. Its colour is excellent camouflage in foliage.

forms an S-shaped loop near the head and sets the curved parts of the body on the ground where they support the weight of the snake. This frictional contact with the ground then allows the animal to stretch its head forward and make another contact, after which the tail is pulled forward. This mode of locomotion can be employed in a tunnel where the S-shaped loop braces the snake against the walls of the tunnel as the head moves forward and a more anterior S is formed so that the tail can be pulled forward. Concertina locomotion is common and it is not unusual to see a snake using both it and lateral undulations at the same time.

The three methods so far described require some sort of fixed points in the form of surface irregularities on the ground, but what if there are none? Suppose the surface gives as the snake exerts pressure against it? If this occurs, any means of locomotion becomes highly inefficient. This problem is encountered by snakes moving over sand, and some have solved it by sidewinding, an almost beautiful sight to watch. During sidewinding, the body of the snake lies at almost a right angle to the direction that the snake is moving. The head is

The Banded slender-neck sea snake *Hydrophis fasciatus* rarely comes ashore. Note the flat, paddle-like tail (to the right).

turned in the direction of movement and lifted forward. As the neck is brought down, the head is still raised and a section of the body behind the point at which the neck contacts the ground is also elevated. At this time, there may be two points at which the snake's body is in stationary contact with the substrate: a point along the neck, and one further back on the body. The neck is then extended forward, and the neck contact shifts backwards, becoming a body contact as the snake's head moves forward as before. The head is brought down, creating a new stationary point at the neck, and the process continues as the snake appears to 'roll' across the ground. The neck is bent at the stationary point and as the head is lifted and carried forward, the body moving behind and the bend moving further back along the body, force is exerted laterally against the ground. If this is sand, it is pushed up on that side and the snake leaves a characteristic hook-shaped track in the sand with the opening of the hook and the 'short side' pointing in the direction of movement, the 'long side' of the hook extending out above and ahead of the opening of the hook at an acute angle to the direction of movement. The whole process is difficult to describe in words and almost as hard to visualize by looking at static drawings or photographs. It is best appreciated, if not understood, as viewed actually

happening or by slow-motion cinematography. It seems that all snakes can sidewind if conditions are appropriate, but it is best developed in some desert vipers such as the Sidewinder rattlesnake *Crotalus cerastes* of the southwestern deserts of North America, and the Horned viper *Cerastes cerastes* of the deserts of the Middle East. Not only do these two snakes sidewind, but they resemble each other almost exactly with the exception that *Cerastes* lacks a rattle. The young of the African viper *Bitis caudalis* uses an extreme variation of the sidewinding mode to escape an intensely hot substrate. The body is thrust forward at such a rate that it completely leaves the ground: the snake jumps!

All snakes can swim, and most have no special locomotor adaptations, but the sea snakes (Hydrophiidae) and wart snakes (Acrochordidae) have. The body is more or less laterally flattened with the tail of sea snakes (for example the Yellow and black sea snake *Pelamus platurus*) becoming paddle-like. Arboreal snakes likewise show some adaptations contributing to their ability to move through vegetation. Many are long, thin snakes with long tails which help in maintaining balance (for example the Vine snake *Oxybelis*, Colubridae), and some of the short, heavy-bodied arboreal species have prehensile tails (for example *Bothrops schlegeli*). Southeast Asia even has 'flying' snakes, members of

Another arboreal snake, the Boomslang *Dispholidus typus* is a rear-fanged species known to be deadly to man. The death of the widely respected American herpetologist Karl P. Schmidt is attributed to a bite by a boomslang. Note the large ventral belly scales.

the colubrid genus *Chrysopelea*, which are reputed to launch themselves from branches and glide for some distance before reaching a lower perch. These snakes seem to have no special modifications, although it is said that the belly is concave as the snake glides, and possibly acts as an air trap as does a parachute. Some of the arboreal snakes are characterized by having long, thin bodies, even thinner necks and tails, and disproportionately large, blunt heads. One such snake is the Blunt-headed tree snake *Imantodes cenchoa* (Colubridae). This snake is capable of extending the forepart of its body inordinately long distances whilst bridging the gap between one branch and another. The usual wide ventral scales are present, but so are enlarged scales on the upper side of the body, the lateral scales being smaller. As the snake extends its body outward, the body is laterally compressed and the result is an I-beam, a structure long known in the construction industry for its rigidity. There are many other adaptations exhibited by snakes for living arboreal lives, and for utilizing other specialized habitats. We will discuss these further in a later chapter.

The Flying snake of southeast Asia *Chrysopelea ornata*, an arboreal species shown gliding from a high branch to a lower one.

Senses

Perception plays an important role in the life of any organism. An animal must be aware not only of the presence of environmental stimuli, but must be able to detect changes in the direction or magnitude of a stimulus. All of an amphibian or reptile's interactions with the environment and with other organisms are dependent upon the presence and sensitivity of sense organs. In this chapter, we will consider only the major senses of vision, hearing, smelling and taste. The sense organs of vertebrates have demonstrated a remarkable constancy. The eye, for example, always assumes generally the same character except in those subterranean organisms which have lost the need for vision and in which the eye has degenerated to some degree or been lost altogether. There has been an elaboration of the ear as terrestrial organisms evolved from aquatic ancestors so that air-borne sounds can be detected, and probably the most dramatic change in the means by which an organism perceives its environment was the shift from dependence on a lateral line system for detecting vibrations travelling through water to dependence on the ear. Jacobson's organ represents a relatively minor addition to the olfactory system if thought of only in terms of the anatomical changes wrought in that system, but the organ is very important in the lives of many lizards and all snakes.

Sight. The differences noted between the eyes of fishes and the eyes of amphibians are associated with the transition from vision through water to vision through air, whereas the differences between the eyes of amphibians and those of reptiles and between different groups of reptiles are accounted for as improvements in the ability of the eye to distinguish images. We have noted earlier that eyelids and mechanisms for lubricating the surface of the eye appeared during metamorphosis of the aquatic larva into a terrestrial adult. The eye itself, however, changes very little and is similar to that of fishes in that the lens is rigid and spherical. Focusing is accomplished by moving the lens forward or backward relative to the light-sensitive (photoreceptor) cells at the back of the eye. Both rods and cones are present among the visual cells. The eyes of frogs are better developed than those of salamanders

as might be expected given the fact that anurans often jump from place to place and need to have good middle-distance vision, and because they must be able to determine the size, distance and speed of prey items which may be flying. The eyes of salamanders are smaller and less well developed and poorly developed in cave-dwelling forms (for example the Olm *Proteus anguineus*, Proteidae, and the Georgia blind salamander *Haideotriton wallacei*, Plethodontidae). Caecilians have very small eyes that lie beneath the skin and are sometimes covered by bone. It is probable that they function only to detect shades of light and dark, not images. All frogs have well developed eyes and no completely cavernicolous species are known although several species are known to enter caves to feed. These species apparently do not venture past the twilight zone near the cave entrance. Eye reduction is known among lizards, snakes and amphisbaenians, but not turtles, rhynchocephalians or crocodilians. It is the burrowing reptiles which have degenerate eyes. The eyes of snakes differ from those of other reptiles, probably because they evolved from the degenerate eyes of burrowing ancestors among the lizards. Aside from anatomical differences between the eyes of snakes and those of other reptiles, there is a difference in the means by which focusing is accomplished. Among snakes, the lens is moved forward or backward as in amphibians, although the mechanism by which this is done is different from that employed by amphibians. Other reptiles focus by changing the shape of the lens. Reptiles as a group have both rod and cone visual cells, but the relative abundance of these differs depending on the degree of nocturnal activity of a given group. Rods, which function to detect differences in light intensity, predominate in nocturnal forms and are the only visual cells in geckos (Gekkonidae) and some of the burrowing snakes. Colour vision is proven for salamanders, turtles, lizards and snakes which are diurnal, and is expected in frogs. Colour vision is accomplished by the cones, and they are the only visual cells present in the eyes of some diurnal lizards and snakes. Colour vision can be important to a diurnal animal in a number of ways, such as in sex determination and food selection. The Desert

A Bullfrog *Rana catesbeiana* displays its large, bulging eyes that afford the animal a wide angle of vision and some degree of binocular vision.

iguana *Dipsosaurus dorsalis* (Iguanidae) is largely herbivorous as an adult and can be maintained in captivity on a diet including fresh lettuce. If given the choice between the green leaves of lettuce and red flower petals, however, the lizard immediately chooses the petals. It can be assumed that the same kind of preferences would be exhibited in nature.

The eyes of nocturnal amphibians and reptiles are usually large, to trap the maximum possible light, and most have a reflecting surface, the tapetum lucidum, behind the rods. Light is reflected back through the visual cells and therefore passes through them twice. The tapetum lucidum is responsible for the eye shine of frogs, crocodilians and other nocturnal animals (including cats and owls) as light is reflected back out of the eye, a fact long recognized by hunters. The pupils of nocturnal amphibians are able to open wide and close down to slits during the day to protect the visual cells from strong light. The vertical pupils of some geckos are serrated along the edges so that when they close a series of tiny holes remain open. Light is thought to pass through these holes to be focused on the same area on the retina. The image so formed would be sharper than that derived from a single opening of the same area as the sum of the holes, and allows the lizard to see well, even in dim light.

Binocular vision improves depth perception and is present to some extent among amphibians and reptiles. Some frogs (for example the Glass frog *Centrolenella*), terrestrial turtles, crocodilians and lizards have limited binocular vision, the visual fields of the two eyes overlapping partially, 25° or less in most, up to about 40° overlap in others. Binocular vision is better developed in some of the reptiles that capture prey with a strike, which implies that they must aim at the prey item and judge its distance. This is true for *Anolis* (Iguanidae), monitor lizards (Varanidae), Snapping turtles (*Chelydra serpentina*, Chelydridae), and some arboreal lizards and snakes. The Tree snake *Ahaetulla mycterizans* (Colubridae) has a horizontally positioned, keyhole-shaped pupil aligned with a groove on the snout. This seems to increase the overlap in the visual fields, and the groove acts somewhat as a sight as well. A number of snake species have lines of contrasting pigment extending in front of the eye, and these may also function as a sight as the animal strikes at prey. Chameleons, of course, can use either monocular or binocular vision, depending upon whether the two eyes are swivelled forward on their turrets to concentrate on a single object or are operated independently when looking at objects in different directions. This same ability is demonstrated by the Cuban 'chameleon' *Chamaeleolis* (Iguanidae) which also resembles true chameleons in form and habits.

The Chameleon *Cham-aeleo pardalis* is able to move each eye independently of the other.

A Third Eye. Amphibians and reptiles possess visual organs other than the lateral eyes on the head. It is known that the skin of at least some amphibians is sensitive to light, but the structures responsible have not been located exactly, nor has the function of light sensitive skin been determined. Much more important and better known is a so-called 'third eye' located at the midline of the head between the lateral eyes. This structure is present in frogs, and especially well-developed in many lizards and the Tuatara where it is clearly visible through one of the scales. In frogs, it appears as a small, nearly colourless spot. The parietal eye is an outgrowth of the hind part of the forebrain, the diencephalon, and was formerly called a pineal end organ or parapineal (among other appellations). The pineal end organ resembles a degenerate eye in reptiles, with visual cells in a retina, a lens and nerve connection to the brain, but it lacks muscles and cannot be focused. A second light-sensitive structure, the pineal body, originates from the same section of the diencephalon as does the pineal end organ, but the pineal body does not develop to resemble a lateral eye. The pineal body is present in all amphibians and remains in reptiles but is less obvious. Neither the pineal end organ nor the pineal body are thought to be capable of forming images, but both can distinguish light from dark. It appears that these structures in amphibians and lizards are important in thermoregulation, because if the structure is blocked in lizards, the animals spend more time in the sun than those which have no block. Blockage also results in the acceleration of the reproductive cycle in lizards. In both amphibians and reptiles, these structures seem important in the establishment of internal rhythms, and in amphibians they may be important in compass orientation.

Hearing. 'Hearing' is accomplished by fishes using the lateral line system. The same system is employed by amphibian larvae, and consists of rows of so-called hair cells in canal systems extending over the body and head as open grooves, as tubes opening to the outside at intervals, or in rows of pits as in amphibians. Each hair cell, or neuromast, has 20–40 hair-like fibres extending from it into the groove, tube or pit and are enervated. As they are bent, by the pressure of low frequency vibrations through the water, a nerve impulse is generated and the animal 'hears'. The lateral line system may function to help the animal maintain equilibrium as well. The system is retained by species which are aquatic as adults, such as the Clawed frog *Xenopus laevis* (Pipidae), some salamanders and caecilians, but lost at metamorphosis by most species. There are exceptions in both directions, so that newts of the genus *Notophthalmus* (Salamandridae) retain the system through the terrestrial eft stage, but this is explained by the fact that these salamanders return to the water to become sexually mature newts after their sojourn on land. Those aquatic amphibians which lack lateral line systems as adults are thought to have evolved their aquatic habits secondarily, having arisen from a terrestrial ancestor.

Hearing by terrestrial organisms, as well as maintenance of balance, is taken over by the ear which can detect the weak vibrations of air that are recognized as sound. Before considering the ear of amphibians and reptiles, we will describe in broad detail the 'typical' vertebrate ear. Sound waves impinge upon some type of external membrane (the 'ear drum' or tympanum), causing it to vibrate

The head of a Golden tree frog *Hyla aurea* clearly shows the external tympanum which is situated behind the eye.

against the chamber behind it, the middle ear. The tympanum is connected by one or more small bones, the ear ossicles, to an opening in the bony capsule surrounding the inner ear. The opening is called the oval window and is much smaller than the tympanum so that the force of vibration is magnified many times. The inner ear contains a fluid, the perilymph, and vibration of the oval window sets up

compression waves in it. These waves are translated across membranes in the inner ear where they impinge upon sensory cells not unlike the hair cells of the lateral line system. All vertebrates have two patches of sensory cells, the macula lagena and the papilla basilaris. Wave action on the sensory hairs causes nerve impulses to be sent to the brain via the acoustic nerve where they are interpreted as sound. This system, oversimplified here, is modified in different groups of amphibians and reptiles.

The ear of most frogs is least modified from that described. There is a large external tympanum which communicates with the inner ear through a single bone, the columella. They and most other living amphibians possess a unique patch of sensory cells in the inner ear called the papilla amphibiorum which are assumed to function in hearing. Among frogs, the middle ear, or the middle ear and columella, or the tympanum are sometimes absent or degenerate. All salamanders lack a tympanum and the columella may be degenerate as well or may be attached to the skull. Caecilians do not have middle ears. They and the salamanders apparently detect vibrations conducted through the ground and transmitted to the inner ear via the lower jaws and fore limbs. The tympanic membrane of 'earless' lizards (for example *Holbrookia*, Iguanidae) is covered by scales and not visible. However, it is visible either on the surface or, in some lizards and crocodilians, lies in a depression. The tympanum of terrestrial turtles and the Tuatara is covered by skin, but its position is usually evident. Snakes have lost the tympanum and middle ear but retain the columella, as do other reptiles, but that bone extends between the oval window of the inner ear and the quadrate bone of the skull rather than a tympanum. Vibrations from the ground are picked up by the lower jaw and transmitted via the quadrate and columella to the inner ear. Sounds may also be transmitted from the air to the quadrate directly and thence to the columella and inner ear. Amphisbaenians lack a tympanum but have a very large columella in the middle ear that articulates with a cartilaginous extracolumella in some species. The extracolumella extends along the lower jaw and is attached to the skin there. Vibrations travel along this pathway to the inner ear. By detecting the relative strength of the vibrations on each side of the head, the amphisbaenian can move toward the source of the noise if it suspects that it has been produced by potential prey.

Hearing does not play a major role in the lives of

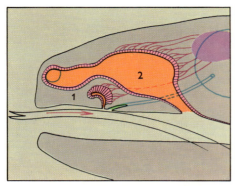

Diagram of the head of a lizard showing Jacobson's organ (1) and the nasal sac (2). Both open into the mouth cavity. Jacobson's organ is visible in the roof of the mouth of the snake shown below.

most amphibians and reptiles relative to the senses of sight and smell, but sound does play a part in predator avoidance, or at least ground vibrations do, and it is important to those frogs which use the call during the breeding season or to stake out territories.

Smell and Taste. The sense of smell, olfaction, is very important to reptiles, less so to amphibians which depend primarily on the sight of moving prey

A Grass snake *Natrix natrix* senses its surroundings with continuous flicks of its tongue.

(or, for burrowing forms, sounds or touch). The nasal passages of amphibians communicate directly into the oral cavity. Part of the passage is lined with olfactory cells, columnar in shape and bearing sensory hairs. The hairs are kept moist by mucous secretions and function in and out of water. The hairs detect air-borne molecules of oderiferous substances and can do so in extremely small amounts. Exactly how they do so is not known. The nasal passages of most reptiles likewise communicate directly into the oral cavity. Jacobson's organs are important in olfaction by lizards and snakes: they open into the nasal passage in amphibians and turtles and are absent in adult crocodilians.

The sense of taste is very closely allied to that of smell. Both are chemosensory in nature. Taste is more important to amphibians, relatively less so among reptiles. The taste buds, which are aggregates of hair cells, are specific in their sensitivity. Each is sensitive to one of four basic tastes: salt, sour, sweet or bitter, and the taste of an item is sensed as a combination of these basic tastes. All of the taste buds look alike and they are restricted to the pharynx in reptiles. Amphibians have taste buds in the skin lining the mouth and tongue, but chemosensory cells are found in the skin of the body as well so that it might be said that amphibians can 'taste' with their skins.

Pit vipers, which belong to the subfamily crotalinae of the family Viperidae and include rattlesnakes and their allies, and some members of the family Boidae (for example *Python*) have a unique type of sense organ for detection of heat. These are the pit organs. In the boids which have them, the pit organs are located in the labial scales, the scales lining the lip, and there may be several organs on each side of the head. The pit organ of viperids is located on the sides of the head between the eyes and the nose. Each pit is lined with a thin membrane containing nerve endings which detect long wave radiation: heat. Experimental studies have revealed that the pit organs can detect a change in temperature of as little as 0·002–0·003°C. They are used to detect the presence of warm-blooded mammals and birds and to direct a strike. A rattlesnake can, using the pit organ, strike quite accurately at a mouse (or a man) in total darkness even if the target is motionless. Boids, of course, hold onto prey items after they have struck, but pit vipers do not and the pit organs make it possible for the snake to trail its dying or disabled prey to where it has collapsed, again in total darkness if necessary.

The head of a pit viper, showing the heat-sensitive pit between eye and nostril and the vertical pupil of this nocturnal snake.

A Forest cobra *Naja melanoleuca* expands its hood when it senses danger.

Colour and Pattern

The particular colour and pattern displayed by any organism, be it plant or animal, is not haphazard. These characteristics of living organisms, when studied in depth, have always been found to be of survival value to the individual and the species to which it belongs. Some of the functions of a colour or colour and pattern combination are obvious, but the functions of others are very subtle and extremely interesting. We will consider both kinds in this chapter. Many of the functions of colour and pattern mentioned, of course, are evident in groups of animals other than amphibians and reptiles.

Amphibian and reptile colours depend on certain characteristics of the skin. Chemical colour results from the absorption by skin pigments of some wavelengths of light and the reflection of others. Skin pigments are contained within cells of the inner layer, the dermis, which are called chromatophores. Four kinds of chromatophores are recognized: melanophores contain black or brown pigments,

The Bearded dragon _Amphibolurus barbatus_ of Australia (left) holds its mouth wide open, its throat pouch inflated to display its beard. The Frilled lizard _Chlamydrosaurus kingii_ (below) exhibits its brightly coloured neck in an alarm-threat display.

lipophores red or yellow pigments, quanophores contain reflective granules or platelets, and allophores contain red, yellow or violet pigments which differ from those of lipophores in certain chemical characteristics. Allophores are never found in amphibians and are rare among reptiles. These chromatophores are stratified in the dermis. The deepest are the melanophores, then come guanophores and lipophores, with allophores at the same

level as the guanophores. The melanophores have extensions called pseudopods and pigment can be dispersed into these or concentrated in the body of the cell. Lipophores can move much as an amoeba moves and may even move beneath the guanophores. Colour can also be determined in part by the structural characteristics of the outer layer of the skin, the epidermis, which may allow some wavelengths of light through and reflect others. This is called physical colour, and the colour of the animal may depend on physical colour, chemical colour, or the combination of the two. Colour changes are effected through the redistribution of pigment within the chromatophores so that it is concentrated or dispersed, and by movements of the lipophores in the vertical plane. These changes are under hormonal control in amphibians, which cannot change colours rapidly, and both hormonal and nervous control in reptiles. Among reptiles, the greater the importance of nervous control, the more rapid the change in colour. The external stimulus for colour change can be light, temperature or interactions with other organisms. A further source of colour in some frogs of the families Centrolenidae, Hylidae and Pseudidae is the presence in the bone, tissues or blood of biliverdin, a green bile pigment.

Camouflage. One important function of colour and pattern for animals is protection in the form of camouflage. Many reptile and amphibian species are cryptically coloured and patterned, that is, the animals are so coloured and patterned as to disappear against their background. This may be done in one of three ways. The animal may match the background, as demonstrated by the hellbender *Cryptobranchus alleganiensis* (Cryptobranchidae)

The bright colours of this West African skink *Riopa fernandii* make the animal conspicuous here but are effective camouflage in its natural habitat.

whose dark spots and blotches on a buff background tend to match the pattern of dark and light areas on the bed of the rivers in which it lives. The Copperhead *Agkistrodon contortrix* (Viperidae) appears boldly coloured with its bands of brown and rust, but against a background of dead leaves it is difficult to see unless it moves. A second form of crypsis finds the animal so coloured and patterned that the outline of its body is obscured against its background. The Copperhead cited above is a good example, as is the Boa constrictor *Boa constrictor* (Boidae). There is a large specimen of the latter in the University of Kansas Museum of Natural History that was captured after the collector, noting movement in the leaves nearby and identifying it as the twitching tail of a boa, traced the body along to where he was standing on the snake's head! Of course, many amphibians and reptiles can change colours to some degree, even if the ability only goes so far as to allow a slight darkening or lightening of the skin. Some reptiles, especially the true chameleons (Chamaeleontidae) are able, however, to change their colouration to a remarkable degree. At least some species of chameleons can match their backgrounds so precisely that different parts of the body are different colours depending upon which

Two colour patterns of the same chameleon, *Chamaeleo lambertoni*, a lizard noted for its ability to change colour to match its background.

This Gaboon viper *Bitis gabonica* is virtually invisible among leaf litter, a classic example of disruptive and concealing colouration.

parts are in the shade and which in the sun. Finally, animals may be countershaded, the upper surfaces usually darker than the lower surfaces. This is evident among many terrestrial species, but is quite pronounced among aquatic species such as the Green sea turtle *Chelonia mydas* (Cheloniidae). A potential predator of a young sea turtle, if searching from above, is peering into the dark depths of the water, and the upper surface of the turtle is dark. If the predator is approaching from below, it is looking up toward a lighter background, the sky, and the lower surface of the turtle is light in colour. Many frogs are similarly pigmented.

It should be apparent that all three means of camouflage just described can work in concert, for a disruptive pattern can, and usually does, match the background upon which the animal is found, and the animal can be countershaded as well. If background matching is important, we might expect to find the colours of a wide-ranging species to demonstrate geographic variation in colour in response to different substrates in different parts of its range. This expectation has been borne out in studies of many different species. The most obvious examples relate to lizards inhabiting white sand or dark lava flow habitats which are much paler or darker, respectively, than populations of the same species found in other habitats. This same pattern is repeated for coat colour of the small rodents living in the dunes and lava flows.

Crypsis is not limited to colour, pattern or morphology. These characteristics of a species might be ineffective if there were no correlated behavioural tendencies on the part of a species. Thus, a Copperhead will be difficult to see if it remains still in the leaves: when it moves it becomes more obvious. The tree frog *Agalychnis callidryas* (Hylidae) has large, bright red eyes and green upper surfaces. The lower surfaces, sides and thighs are differently coloured and patterned. During the day, when these frogs are asleep on leaves, the limbs are pulled in toward the body and the eyes closed, making them appear as inconspicuous green lumps on a green background. Other sleeping postures might expose the contrasting colours of the sides and thighs, making the frogs more obviously visible to a diurnal predator.

Venomous Species. Rather than attempt to avoid discovery, some species actually call attention to themselves by a combination of bright colour and activity. Such amphibians and reptiles are usually noxious in some way, either in taste as perceived by a predator, or in being venomous. Among amphibians, the poison dart frogs (Dendrobatidae) and members of the bufonid genus *Atelopus* are examples, as is the terrestrial eft stage in the life cycle of the newt *Notophthalmus viridescens* (Salamandridae). Skin glands of these species secrete highly toxic substances. All are diurnal, and all are brightly coloured. Efts are bright reddish-orange to orange, and the frogs cited are extremely variable in both colour and pattern, but reds, blues, greens and black are encountered. These are warning (aposematic) colours. A naive predator might capture one of these conspicuous amphibians, but the toxic secretions would cause it to quickly release the captive. Experiments have shown that one or two bad experiences are enough to teach a bird to avoid further encounters with one of these noxious amphibians.

Some venomous reptiles are also brilliantly coloured. The Gila monster *Heloderma suspectum* (Helodermatidae) has a bold pattern of black or brown markings separated by patches of orange or pinkish pigment. Both highly venomous coral snakes (*Micrurus* and *Micruroides*, Elapidae) and mildly venomous, rear-fanged snakes (for example *Erythrolamprus*, Colubridae) may be aposematic. Species of the genera cited are noted for their bright patterns of red, black and yellow bands. It seems probable that, in these snakes at least, this colour

pattern has multiple functions. Although the snakes stand out against a uniform background, they are difficult to see in their natural habitat and the colour pattern may be to that extent cryptic. The coral snakes are highly venomous, and it is difficult to imagine a predator, a bird for example, learning anything from an encounter with one. The bird would either kill the snake without being bitten and learn nothing about avoiding such brightly coloured snakes, or be bitten and die. But, in spite of this, it has recently been found that the tendency to avoid coral snake patterns may be inherited. Thus, hand-reared motmots (tropical birds and potential snake predators) avoided cylindrical wooden models painted with the coral snake pattern, but attacked models with green and blue rings or with red and yellow stripes.

Mimicry. The concept of mimicry has always been controversial, and especially so with reference to

Bright colours sometimes act as warning signals, as in the case of this frog, *Dendrobates*, which has poison-secreting glands in its skin.

amphibians and reptiles. Basically, the idea is this: if a harmless organism looks and acts like a noxious one, predators which learn to avoid the noxious species will simultaneously learn to avoid the other. The noxious or venomous species is the model in such a complex, the imitator a mimic. For this to work, the model should be more abundant than the mimic. Otherwise, a predator would have a greater probability of encountering the edible mimic instead of the model and might not learn to avoid either. This has been termed Batesian mimicry after H. W. Bates, the English naturalist who first described it over 100 years ago on the basis of his observations on tropical butterflies. Most of the recent studies of Batesian mimicry in amphibians have revolved around two model-mimic complexes. In one of these, the edible red mud salamanders *Pseudotriton* (Plethodontidae) are said to mimic the noxious red eft described above. In the other, the model is the Red-cheeked salamander *Plethodon jordani jordani*, that is mimicked by red, orange or yellow-cheeked variants of the Mountain dusky salamander *Desmognathus ochrophaeus carolinensis*. Both of the latter are plethodontids. It has been shown that certain predators, such as Blue jays, avoid the models after exposure, but will eat the mimics if not exposed to the model first. Criticism has been

levelled at these findings because most of the predators tested have been diurnal, whereas it is often asserted that the salamanders are nocturnal and therefore unavailable to day-active predators. Recently, however, it has been demonstrated that the supposedly nocturnal salamanders are, in fact, often active during the day. The question has not been resolved, but alternative explanations for the similarities that exist between at least the red-cheeked salamanders have been suggested. For example, the physiological processes that result in a red-cheek might also confer some advantage to the organism in the environment in which it lives. It would be this advantage that is promoted in an evolutionary sense (by natural selection), and the cheek-patch merely follows along. If the model and its mimic are found in similar habitats (which they are), then they might both have evolved the same physiological processes and, therefore, might both have cheek-patches.

Batesian mimicry has also been proposed as an explanation for the similarity between the venomous coral snakes and such harmless snakes that occur with them as the Milk snake *Lampropeltis triangulum* of the eastern United States, and the tropical American snakes *Pliocercus elapoides* and *Simophis rhinostoma* (all colubrids). The range of

The Ribbon snake *Thamnophis sauritus* on the edge of Okefenokee swamp, United States. Its longitudinal markings make it resemble a Garter snake. This is an example of coincidence, however, not Batesian mimicry, because Garter snakes are harmless.

the Milk snakes overlaps that of the coral snake *Micrurus fulvius*, and where the snakes occur together, they are very similar. Outside this area, the pattern of the Milk snake is less like that of a coral snake, becoming blotched instead of banded. The Mexican king snake *Lampropeltis triangulum gaigae* resembles the coral snake with which it occurs as a juvenile, when both are about the same size, but as it grows to a larger size than the coral snake it becomes completely black or nearly so. *Pliocercus* populations are characterized by colour patterns that resemble those of coral snakes of the area, and parallel changes in pattern occur over the coincident ranges of the two kinds of snakes. Something similar to the situation seen in the relationship between Milk snakes and the Eastern coral snake is found in the *Plethodon jordani jordani-Desmognathus ochrophaeus carolinensis* complex, in that the latter species does not have a cheek patch outside the areas it shares with *P. jordani*.

Two other kinds of mimicry have been described, both of which find examples among the snakes. The first of these, Müllerian mimicry, involves complexes where all species are noxious. A predator learning or having the innate ability to avoid one member of the complex tends to avoid all members of the complex. This concept applies to complexes of tropical American snakes. Finally, if predators do not have the inherited ability to avoid coral snake patterns, Mertensian mimicry might come into play. Proposed by Wolfgang Wickler, Mertensian mimics are both harmless snakes and lethally poisonous ones; the models are mildly poisonous species which would make a predator sick if bitten, but not kill it, thus allowing for learning to occur.

Some species of amphibians and reptiles are cryptic in dorsal colour and pattern, but brightly coloured ventrally. The ventral colouration, though not normally visible, may be employed to startle a potential predator. Some of the tree frogs (Hylidae) such as *Agalychnis callidryas* which was mentioned above, use the brightly pigmented colours along their sides as flash colours. If disturbed by a predator, the frog leaps and the sides are exposed. The predator catches just a glimpse of bright colouration and may continue to look for it after the frog has landed and assumed a posture covering the sides with the limbs. The predator may completely miss the frog, which now sits cryptically within easy reach. The Fire-bellied toad *Bombina bombina* (Discoglossidae) is darkly pigmented above, but bright orange below. If the animal is molested, it arches its back and turns

the hands and feet upward, exposing the lower surfaces while closing its eyes and remaining rigid. This is called an unken reflex and is another way of advertising the noxious nature of the frog.

Behaviour Involving the Tail. Mimics in model-mimic complexes practise deception to avoid predation. Other forms of deception are employed by some reptiles. One such deception involves a tail display and is used by certain snakes and amphisbaenians. If the snake is touched, the head is hidden, sometimes in coils of the body, and the tail held in a manner which mimics the head. The tails of some such snakes are blunt and rounded; of others, pointed, sometimes with a sharp terminus. Many of

This defensive manoeuvre does not involve bright colours as does the unken reflex described in the text. Here a European common toad *Bufo bufo* confronts a Grass snake, *Natrix natrix*. By puffing itself up and rising high on its legs, it prevents the predator from swallowing it.

the species have tails which are distinct in colour from the body or which are brightly coloured ventrally. Bright ventral colouration might make the snake's tail look like a head with an open mouth as it is waved about, an idea supported by the fact that the ventral colouration is usually red or yellow. Tail display might serve several functions which are not mutually exclusive. The display could direct the attack of a predator away from the head and toward the tail, which can sustain more damage than the head without killing the snake. It could also be employed as an intimidation device or, for those species with brightly coloured ventral surfaces, as a startle device to disorientate potential predators. The display might also be a form of behavioural mimicry. Coral snakes of the genus *Micrurus* all employ tail displays and these may be mimicked by species of *Pliocercus* which also mimic them in colour and pattern. It has been suggested that the tail display of *Amphisbaena alba* (Amphisbaenidae) may induce a predator to attack the tail and provide a directional stimulus for a counterattack by this nearly blind reptile. It has also been suggested that the displays might promote an attack toward an offensive cloacal discharge, as in a Sand boa *Eryx tataricus*, or to a tail which can be autotomized (see below).

Snakes may sometimes employ the tail as a lure. This has been confirmed for a number of species of viperids which, as juveniles or adults or throughout life, have tails with colours that contrast with the body. Thus *Bothro bilineatus* coils with its tail held erect and twitching. *Anolis* lizards are attracted to the tail, attempt to attack it and are themselves eaten by the snake. The body of *B. bilineatus* is pale green with a yellow stripe on each side, but the slightly swollen tail is pinkish.

Lizards may use a contrastingly coloured tail in a different manner. Many such species have modifications of the tail vertebrae that enable the tail to be autotomized, that is broken at the will of the lizard in response to stress, or as a result of being pulled. The fracture plane is within the vertebrae, not between them. After the tail breaks off, the fragment continues to jump and twitch and may divert the attention of a predator as the lizard escapes. An alternative hypothesis to explain contrasting body and tail colouration, which is often seen in juvenile lizards but disappears as the animal ages, has been suggested by those who object to the idea that the brightly coloured (often blue) tail functions primarily to divert an attack to the tail. They point out

that a cryptically coloured tail would have made the animal less visible to the predator in the first place, and because the diversion hypothesis does not account for the loss of a contrasting tail colouration with age. These investigators suggest that the tail colouration is a visual stimulus inhibiting attacks by males of the same species. They exposed adult male Five-lined skinks *Eumeces fasciatus* (Scincidae) to juvenile lizards which had complete, bright blue tails and to juveniles which had their tails removed. The males were much more likely to attack the individuals that lacked a blue tail than those with the tail. It seems likely that the diversion hypothesis and the attack inhibition hypothesis are not mutually exclusive although one or the other may be more important in explaining the origin of the brightly coloured tails in such lizards.

Internal Colouration. Diurnal amphibians and reptiles are often found to have the surface lining of the body cavity, the peritoneum, heavily pigmented with black. This pigmentation is often limited to the area over or around the gonads. The black pigment is melanin. Nocturnal or cavernicolous (cave-dwelling) organisms lack this black peritoneum, whereas diurnal desert-dwelling species exhibit it to the greatest degree. It has been suggested that the pigmentation protects the gonads of these animals from ultraviolet light which can penetrate through the skin unless the skin itself is heavily pigmented. It has been found that the intensity and wavelengths of light which penetrate the body cavity of a lizard can be mutagenic. That is, the light can cause mutations or other damage to the reproductive cells. Nocturnal species or those not exposed to high intensity sunlight would have no need for the protection afforded by a black peritoneum. Colour change in the Desert iguana *Dipsosaurus dorsalis* (Iguanidae) may be a factor affecting radiation protection. The Desert iguana has limited powers of colour change, but it can darken and lighten somewhat. In the dark phase, considerably less radiation in the form of light passes through the body wall than in the light phase, as much of it is absorbed by the dark skin. In the light phase, which the animal maintains in order to warm to its preferred body temperature, potentially mutagenic (mutation-causing) doses of radiation would reach the gonads if there were no black peritoneum.

Colour can also be an important factor in the thermoregulation of an amphibian or reptile. As indicated above, dark skin absorbs radiation and causes the animal to warm up. Light skin reflects radiation and decreases the rate at which body temperatures rise. Consequently, desert lizards are darker as they emerge from their burrows in the morning and while they bask before commencing foraging activities. As they gain heat, they become lighter. There may be a critical temperature at which colour change begins. There is, of course, a limit on how light or dark a given lizard species can become, and much amphibian and reptilian thermoregulation is behavioural. As they become too warm, they simply retreat into the shade until the body temperature declines. Species which cannot change colour are restricted in their activity patterns to nocturnal or crepuscular (dawn or dusk) periods, or are subterranean for the most part. It is worth noting that the colour changes associated with thermoregulation are also important in background matching for some species. Thus, the Desert iguana is better able to match the sand upon which it is active when it is in the light phase, the phase at which it is within the thermal range which permits normal activity. Finally, it should be pointed out that crypsis is, somewhat surprisingly, the primary function of colour in some species even in desert environments. It has been shown that seven species of rattlesnakes in a desert habitat near Phoenix, Arizona, responded in an identical manner to radiation, regardless of their colour, and thermoregulation seemed to depend more on conduction of heat from the ground.

The Red-banded frogs *Phrynomerus bifasciatus* of Africa are unusual in losing their bright colours in strong sunlight.

Sometimes we find apparent paradoxes as we examine animal colour. A good example is afforded by the melanistic (black) lizards *Ameiva* (Teiidae) which occur on a few scattered islands in the Caribbean and similarly pigmented *Lacerta* (Lacertidae) on islands in the Aegean Sea. *Ameiva corvina* on the island of Sobrero, for example, is totally black yet the island is white limestone, causing the animal to stand out conspicuously against its background. Melanism is unknown in this genus on the mainland and on most of the islands which it inhabits, apparently because such habitats have predators which feed on lizards. Sombrero and the other islands supporting populations of melanistic lizards lack such predators, so melanism is tolerated. Even though it is tolerated, we can still ask why the lizards are not normally pigmented. Apparently melanism plays a thermoregulatory role. By being able to warm up rapidly, the lizards can be active earlier in the day and have longer activity periods than normally pigmented relatives. This may be important on these islands, which are quite barren and where food is hard to come by. An additional period during which foraging can occur would be a distinct advantage. There may be other advantages, but research on this topic is in its embryonic stages. Melanism is also found in some lizards living at high elevations, such as the Andean *Liolaemus* (Iguanidae), where it contributes to thermoregulation.

Colour and pattern are of obvious importance in reproductive activities of amphibians and reptiles, where they may be important as reproductive isolating mechanisms between species and as cues in courtship behaviour. We have seen an example of this as we reviewed the reproductive behaviour of the Rainbow lizard *Agama agama*, and in the same chapter, we saw that colour can be important in sex recognition (for example eye colour in the Box turtles *Terrapene carolina*). In the examples we cited, the common pattern was for males to adopt breeding colours whereas the female signalled her readiness to breed by her behaviour and not by colour changes. There is an example of a breeding colour change by a female lizard, but the change occurs *after* mating. At this time, female Leopard lizards *Gambelia* (or *Crotaphytus*) *wislizenii* develop red spots on the flanks. No such colour change is evident among males. One hypothesis explaining this is that this colour pattern inhibits further courtship by other males, courtship behaviour that would in a sense be wasted because the female has already mated.

107

Adaptations for Life in Specific Habitats

Much of this book has been devoted to discussions of the ways amphibians and reptiles have become adapted for life in different kinds of habitats. There are a number of such adaptations which do not comfortably fit under any of the previous chapter headings, and we will consider these here. Rather than take a taxonomic approach, discussing amphibians first, then reptiles, we will first examine some adaptations for an aquatic or semiaquatic existence, with the emphasis on reptiles. Then we will describe some of the ways amphibians and reptiles cope with arid environments. Finally, some further adaptations of burrowing reptiles will be discussed.

The Aquatic Habitat. Aside from strictly locomotor adaptations that have already been discussed, turtles and crocodilians exhibit some other interesting characteristics relative to the degree to which they are aquatic. The first of these is shape. Terrestrial turtles, such as most box turtles *Terrapene* (Emydidae) and the various land tortoises of the family Testudinidae (for example *Geochelone*, *Gopherus* and *Testudo*), have high-vaulted dorsal shells. The more aquatic turtles, if only swimming species are considered, have more streamlined shapes. Thus, the South American river turtle *Podocnemis expansa* (Pelomedusidae) and the New Guinea long-necked turtle *Chelodina novae-guinae* (Chelyidae) have very low dorsal shells. The Coahuila box turtle *Terrapene coahuilae*, an endangered species, is highly aquatic for a box turtle and its carapace is noticeably lower than that of its more terrestrial relatives. The most streamlined turtles are the soft shelled turtles (for example *Trionyx*, Trionychidae and *Carettochelys*, Carettochelyidae) and the sea turtles (Cheloniidae and

A Hawksbill turtle *Eretmochelys imbricata*, showing how the limbs have been modified to flippers to make aquatic life possible.

The European Pond tortoise *Emys orbicularis* spends most of its time in water but does not have limbs modified as flippers.

Dermochelyidae). The former are very flat. The soft dorsal shell of *Trionyx* has an almost knife-like edge. The latter have fusiform (tear-drop) outlines as viewed from the side. *Trionyx* has some interesting respiratory adaptations as well. The snout is long and tapered and the neck is quite long so that, as the turtle lies beneath the surface of the water, just the tip of the snout can be extended above water-level for breathing. The lining of the cloaca and the oral cavity is highly vascularized in *Trionyx*, and some oxygen can be obtained directly from the water, allowing the animal to remain completely submerged for a very long time. Bottom-walking turtles, such as the Snapping turtle *Chelydra serpentina* (Chelydridae), the musk turtles *Sternothaerus* (Kinosternidae) and the Matamata *Chelys fimbriata* (Chelyidae), do not have such streamlined shapes as those aquatic turtles which spend considerable periods of time swimming. These turtles have more highly vaulted dorsal shells and they are often ornamented in various way to help camouflage the turtle on the bottom. The rough shells of these turtles also provide a substrate on which algae can grow, and these provide further camouflage, deceiving both the predators and the prey of these turtles.

In addition to shell shape, the relative buoyancy of terrestrial and aquatic turtles differs. Comparison can be made using the so-called 'sinking factor', which is weight of an object divided by its volume (=its specific gravity), this quotient then being multiplied by 1,000. Turtles with sinking factors of less than 1,000 float, those with sinking factors greater than 1,000 sink. The specific gravity of water is 1·000, so a turtle with a sinking factor of 1,000 would neither sink nor float but remain at whatever depth it found itself without expending energy to do so. Aquatic turtles have a sinking factor greater than 1,000. That for the Painted turtle *Chrysemys scripta*

(Emydidae) is 1,108; for the Spiny softshell *Trionyx spinifer* (Trionychidae) it is 1,076. The Eastern box turtle *Terrapene carolina* (Emydidae) has a sinking factor of only 760 and is terrestrial. Its more aquatic relative, *T. coahuila*, has a sinking factor of 960. This betrays the partially terrestrial tendencies in the ancestors of *T. coahuila* and is paralleled by some of the other turtles which are primarily terrestrial but frequently enter the water. An example is Blanding's turtle *Emydoidea blandingi* (Emydidae) which has a sinking factor of 978. Bottom-walkers have sinking factors very close to 1,000, probably because they do not swim very much. If they had a sinking factor much lower, they would have to expend greater amounts of energy to remain on the bottom and

would have a tendency to float. Were their sinking factors much higher, they would have to work harder to reach the surface to breathe.

Crocodilians also exhibit an array of adaptations for a semiaquatic life aside from strictly locomotor adaptations such as having a strong, keeled tail. These reptiles spend a great deal of time floating just beneath the surface. Both the nostrils and eyes, as well as the ears, are elevated to the same level so that they just project above the surface when the animal is afloat. The nostrils and ears are provided with valves and can be closed off as the animal dives. Both upper and lower eyelids are present, as is a transparent membrane, the nictitating membrane, which can be moved over the eye when the animal is submerged, protecting it while allowing continued vision. The jaws of crocodilians cannot be closed tightly enough to exclude water, and this would make it impossible for most reptiles to breathe with the mouth under water even though the nostrils were held above the surface. But they do breathe, and this is made possible by the presence of a secondary palate which separates the passages from the mouth cavity. Crocodilians are thus able to breathe, even though the mouth is full of water.

Life at Sea. There are no marine amphibians although some populations of frogs and salamanders are known which live in brackish (semi-salty) water or in 'splash zones' near the shore. These species have not yet been extensively studied. Several marine reptiles are known, and they exhibit some special adaptations for life at sea. All possess a salt gland for ridding the body of excess salt. This is a nasal gland in lizards and is found in representatives of a number of lizard families. The gland is very large in the Marine iguana *Amblyrhynchus cristatus* (Iguanidae), and extends well over the eyes with the duct opening into the front nasal sac. Turtle salt glands are found behind the eye and are called lachrymal salt glands. They too are not restricted to marine turtles. The Diamondback terrapin *Malaclemys terrapin* (Emydidae), which inhabits salt marshes and is, incidentally, the usual ingredient in turtle soup as served in Chinese restaurants, has a well-developed lachrymal gland. Snakes which enter saline habitats have salt glands located under and around the tongue sheath and are called posterior sublingual salt glands. They are found in sea snakes

Like the softshelled turtle, this Matamata *Chelys fimbriata* uses its elongate proboscis like a snorkel. It can remain almost fully submerged and concealed while breathing. Some oxygen is also obtained directly from the water via the well-vascularized walls of the throat.

This Black caiman *Melano-suchus niger* from the Amazon Basin of South America illustrates several aquatic adaptations of crocodilians. Note that the eyes and nostrils are raised, enabling the reptile to lie nearly submerged with only these structures exposed. The nostrils and ear opening, the horizontal slit behind the eye, are valvular and can be closed as the caiman submerged.

(Hydrophiidae) and the File snake *Acrochordus granulatus* (Acrochordidae). Salt glands are also known in marine birds, such as sea gulls, and they, and those turtles and lizards which have salt glands, may sometimes be seen to have an encrustation of salt around the nose (in lizards and birds) or beneath the eye (in turtles). Drops of salty fluid have been found on the sides of aquaria containing sea snakes.

An additional word must be said about sea snakes. Many have bodies that taper, sometimes rather abruptly (for example in *Microcephalophis gracilis*), so that the front part of the body, while elongate, is not so thick as the hind part. This may be an adaptation for striking at prey while suspended in water. You may be aware of the law of physics which states that every action must have an equal and opposite reaction. And you may have felt a practical result of that law if you have ever fired a rifle and felt the 'kick' against your shoulder. If a sea snake strikes at a fish, the forward force of the strike would tend to push the snake backwards and thereby reduce the force of the strike. A terrestrial snake, braced against the ground, doesn't have this problem. One way to reduce the magnitude of the problem would be to increase the mass of the hind part of the body so that the head of the snake can thrust forward against this greater mass.

Marine iguanas have evolved an equally innovative means of handling a problem in thermoregulation as they swim in the cold waters of the Humboldt current off the Galapagos Islands. These lizards must dive directly from the warm rocks upon

Another view of the Black caiman *Melanosuchus niger* shows the long tail that makes powerful swimming possible.

The Galapagos marine iguana *Amblyrhynchus cristatus* is the only lizard that habitually enters the sea, which it does to feed on seaweed.

which they bask, into the cold waters in which they feed on seaweed. They require some mechanism to prevent over rapid cooling, which would greatly limit the time they could spend in the water and the distance they could forage from the rocks. Also, they need a mechanism to permit rapid warming once they leave the water. They have solved both problems by adjusting the heart rate so that it is more rapid when the animal is heating than when it is cooling. Ashore, the lizards maintain a body temperature of about 98°F (37°C), and the water is 18–27°F (10–15°C) cooler. When the heart rate is low, blood travels less rapidly between the surface of the body and the core, and so the core is cooled relatively slowly. When the rate is high, as when the animal is heating on the warm rocks, the blood coursing through the surface vessels is warmed and carried to the core rapidly, thus increasing the rate at which the whole animal warms up.

Arid Habitats. Let us now shift our attention to amphibians and reptiles inhabiting arid regions. An enormous amount of work has been done on the biologies of these animals and much more is known about them than about species inhabiting, for example, the wet tropics. Much more remains to be learned. Amphibians and reptiles of the desert face a potentially hostile world from a thermoregulatory standpoint. As ectotherms, they cannot regulate their body temperatures internally by metabolic means. The greatest powers in that direction exhibited by reptiles are those of the Marine iguana discussed above. Most desert amphibians and reptiles simply avoid the problem by being nocturnal or crepuscular. However, some species are active during daylight hours. These animals, all reptiles if we consider only terrestrial species, thermoregulate partially by behavioural means. A good example is afforded by the Horned lizard *Phrynosoma* (Iguanidae) which spends the cool desert nights buried in the sand. As the sun rises, the lizard sticks its head out of the sand and total emergence and activity seem dependent upon head temperature. Once the critical temperature has been achieved, the Horned lizard emerges to begin its day's activities. It can lower its body temperature by the simple expediency of entering the shade, and raise it by moving into the sun. If it becomes too hot, the lizard will flatten the body by spreading the ribs and orient itself parallel to the sun's rays, so that they strike the edge of the flattened body, and exposure is minimal. If, on the other hand, the lizard's body temperature drops below a critical level, the body is turned so that the sun's rays strike it at right angles and exposure is maximal. If the lizard is prevented from reaching shade and cannot cool sufficiently by posturing alone, it pants and cooling is effected by evaporative means as the moist lining of the mouth is exposed. All of these mechanisms are utilized by desert lizards, and they are often accompanied (as in the Horned lizard) by changes in colour which are themselves thermoregulatory. Some of these adaptations allow the lizards to remain active and feeding longer than if they had to depend entirely on movements in and out of shade.

Desert amphibians, and that may seem almost a contradiction, are nocturnal unless restricted to permanent bodies of water. Water availability is a much more important factor in their lives than temperature. A number of adaptations have evolved to reduce the rate of water loss or allow rapid rehydration should the animal become dehydrated. As there are few terrestrial salamanders and no caecilians in deserts, our discussion will centre around anurans. In general, it is probably true that dry-adapted species of frogs are more tolerant of water loss than are inhabitants of more moist habitats. Thus the Western spadefoot *Scaphiopus hammondi* (Pelobatidae) will tolerate a loss in body weight of nearly 50% due to dehydration whereas the aquatic Pig frog *Rana grylio* (Ranidae) will only tolerate a loss of just over 30%. Arid zone species may also rehydrate more rapidly than species from wetter regions and a study of four species of the Australian genus *Neobatrachus* (Myobatrachidae) revealed rehydration rates in agreement with the degree of aridity in their habitats. The same study found no such correlation for species of the genus *Heleioporus* (another Australian myobatrachid), so the picture is not clear cut. Anurans such as *Bufo* (Bufonidae) and *Scaphiopus* can rehydrate to some extent by merely sitting on an area of moist sand. The lower surface of the frog is thin and highly vascularized, and moisture can be absorbed directly through skin: the frog essentially has an absorptive 'seat-patch'. Desert anurans (and turtles) can also make use of bladder water if other sources are unavailable because water stored in the bladder can move through the bladder walls, back into the body. The so-called Australian Water-holding frog *Cyclorana platycephalus* (Myobatrachidae) can hold fluid equal to 50% of the weight of the frog! Recently it has been discovered that a few arid zone frogs

Many snakes are able to swim but show few adaptations for aquatic life. The Egyptian cobra *Naja haje* is shown here.

The Sungazer *Cordylus giganteus*, like many lizards adapted for life in hot climates, is covered with spiny, bony plates that underlie the scales.

excrete uric acid instead of urea. Uric acid, the primary means of ridding the body of nitrogenous wastes in reptiles, is not toxic and requires little water for excretion. Less water is lost by excreting uric acid than by excreting urea as is the case among most adult amphibians. Finally, some of the hylid tree frogs inhabiting arid regions couple an unusual morphological feature with an even more unusual behaviour to escape desiccation. Members of the genera *Aparasphenodon*, *Trachycephalus*, *Triprion*, and *Pternohyla* have co-ossified skulls, that is, the skin on the head is fused to the bone beneath. The skulls of these and other such species are often heavily ornamented with crests, ridges and flanges, so these frogs have come to be called casque-headed hylids. The species cited exhibit a behaviour called phragmosis: they use their heads to fill cavities or block holes. *Pternohyla* uses its head to plug the entrance to its burrow whereas the other genera, which are arboreal, use the head to plug tree holes or holes in terrestrial bromeliads (the plant group to which pineapple belongs). By so plugging the

chamber in which the frog rests with the solid and non-vascular head, moisture levels within the chamber remain high. Another benefit of the behaviour is that the entrances to the burrows are camouflaged at the same time.

Burrowing. Burrowing reptiles face some problems we have not yet considered, especially if they are inhabitants of deserts or other areas where the ground is composed of relatively loose sand. True tunnels may not be formed in dry, loose sand, because the sand will tend to close in after the animal has passed through and will, in fact, tend to collapse around the animal as it burrows or lies concealed. As such an animal breathes, one might expect that sand would press against it as exhalation occurs, and that the weight of this sand would have to be lifted as the animal inhaled. One might also expect sand grains to be sucked into the nasal passages and thence into the mouth cavity and lungs if they weren't trapped in the passages, plugging them. And, as the animal burrowed through the loose sand, loose grains should force their way between the closed lips and

114

The Thorny devil *Moloch horridus* of the arid regions of Australia. The function of the spines is not known for certain, but they probably serve to ward off predators.

into the mouth. All of these things *might* occur, but in well-adapted sand-burrowers, such as the fringe-toed lizard *Uma* (Iguanidae) they do not. The respiratory movements of the Desert iguana *Dipsosaurus dorsalis* (Iguanidae) has been compared with those of the sand-burrowing or sand-swimming iguanid genera *Uma*, *Callisaurus* (gridiron-tailed lizards) and *Holbrookia* (earless lizards). As the Desert iguana breathes, the pressure changes necessary to fill and empty the lungs are produced by expansion and contraction of the rib cage. As expiration occurs, the rib cage is compressed laterally. In the sand-burrowers, breathing is accomplished by vertical movements of the belly so that it is concave on expiration, flat on inspiration. Sand does not fill in under the lizard as it exhales, and so the belly is not required to displace any sand as the lizard inhales. Similar breathing movements are employed by a number of lizard species and by the Burrowing boa *Eryx johni* (Boidae), as well as by some species of lizards which have flattened bodies and seek shelter in crevices (for example Yarrow's

spiny lizard *Sceloporus jarrovi*, Iguanidae). *Eryx johni* and *E. conicus* both breathe by lateral compression at the surface, and *E. conicus* continues to do so when buried. Its position is revealed by sand movements above it as it lies $\frac{1}{10}-\frac{3}{10}$ in (3–4 mm) deep, but no such movements betray the position of *E. johni*. Two mechanisms prevent sand from passing through or clogging the nasal passages of *Uma*. First, the passage is U-shaped and functions like a sink trap. Sand may reach the bottom of the 'U', but it travels no further before being expelled as the lizard exhales. Secondly, if the lizard is slightly warmer than the surrounding sand when it comes to rest, water vapour in the air it exhales will condense on sand grains around the nostrils forming a pack of moist sand which does not collapse or release loose sand into the nostrils. Finally, the jaws of *Uma* are, like those of most sand-swimmers, constructed so that the lower jaws nests in the upper jaw when closed. With the lower jaw countersunk in this manner, sand cannot be forced so easily between the lips as it could if the lips simply abutted one another.

115

picta

Seattle

oregonensis

platensis

xanthoptica

San Francisco

croceator

eschscholtzi

klauberi

Los Angeles

Regions of intermediate forms

1 Between *oregonensis* and *picta*

2 between *oregonensis* and *xanthoptica*
In the coastal region and between
oregonensis and *platensis* in the Sierra Nevada

3 between *xanthoptica* and *eschscholtzi*

4 between *platensis* and *croceator*

5 between *croceator* and *klauberi*

6 between *xanthoptica* and *platensis* with
partial inbreeding

7 between *eschscholtzi* and *klauberi* without
interbreeding

Zoogeography is the study of the geographic distribution of animals. With its sister science, plant geography, it makes up the broader discipline of biogeography. In this chapter, we will discuss the present distribution patterns of amphibians and reptiles on a broad scale, at the order, suborder and family levels, and try to account for how certain groups of amphibians and reptiles have come to occupy the geographic ranges that they do. Sometimes this will involve consideration of geological events, at other times we will want to discuss the tolerances of the organisms with respect to environmental variables such as temperature or salinity, or characteristics of the organisms that foster dispersal, or interactions between species, including man. We will begin by describing the broad global distributions of the major groups of amphibians and reptiles.

World Distribution Patterns. Among the amphibians, caecilians are the most restricted in their distribution. Most are found only in the wet tropics of Africa, the Oriental Region, and Middle and South America. They have reached few islands, although they are found in the Indonesian Archipelago as far east as Bali and, surprisingly, in the Seychelles in the Indian Ocean. Salamanders, on the other hand, are primarily north temperate in distribution, descending into the tropics only in the New World where one group of lungless salamanders (Plethodontidae) have been successful as far south as the Amazon Basin. Salamanders are restricted in their insular distribution to islands on the continental shelf (continental islands) such as those of Japan and the British Isles. Although limited in their southern distribution, salamanders have been reasonably successful at high latitudes in the north. The record is probably held by *Hynobius keyserlingii* (Hynobiidae) which ranges north of the Arctic Circle in Siberia where winter temperatures are about 100°F (66°C) lower than summer temperatures. Frogs as a group are by far the most widely distributed of amphibians, partly because they have successfully colonized islands the world over. In the western hemisphere, frogs have been found from Tierra del Fuego in the south to above the Arctic Circle in western North America (Wood frog *Rana*

sylvatica, Ranidae). In the eastern hemisphere, they range from the southern limits of land in Africa, Tasmania and New Zealand to at least 71°N latitude in Scandinavia (Common frog *Rana temporaria*, Ranidae). Whereas only one species of salamander, and no caecilians, approach or cross the Arctic Circle, several frog species do, including species of tree frogs (*Hyla*) and chorus frogs (*Pseudacris*), both hylids, and toads of the genus *Bufo* (Bufonidae).

Of the orders and suborders of reptiles, the Rhynchocephalia has the most restricted range. The only living representative, the Tuatara *Sphenodon punctatus*, occurs only on a few small islands off New Zealand. Relatives of the Tuatara were, however, much more widely distributed in the past as evidenced by fossils from the Upper Triassic to Upper Cretaceous of Europe, South Africa, southeast Asia and North America. The Tuatara lives close to the southern limit of distribution for reptiles; few others tolerate the climatic conditions in which the Tuatara thrives. Reptiles in general favour warmer climates. The crocodilians are essentially pan-tropical in distribution, with various genera and species distributed around the world at low latitudes. The American and Chinese alligators

If a species has a large range, populations in different parts of that range may evolve differences in response to differing environments (left). The North American Wood frog *Rana sylvatica* (below) ranges further north than any other North American amphibian or reptile.

(*Alligator mississipiensis* and *A. sinensis*, respectively) are more cool-tolerant than other crocodilians as they range into the north temperate zone. Many crocodilians tolerate sea water quite well and several have been found off shore. It is easy to see how they have included many of the larger, near-shore islands within their range. Amphisbaenians are also primarily tropical although the fossil record indicates that they were once more widely distributed in North America and Europe. Today they occur in Africa, South America and the West Indies, with one genus (*Rhineura*) found in Florida, one in western Mexico (*Bipes*), one in Spain (*Blanus*), and several in Turkey, Asia Minor and certain coastal and oceanic islands.

The other major groups of reptiles, the turtles, lizards and snakes, are much more widely distributed on a global scale. All occur in the tropics but are well-represented in temperate climates as well. In the north, only two turtles reach or exceed 50° north latitude. The European swamp turtle *Emys orbicularis* (Emydidae) ranges to at least 57°N, and the

Horned lizards, *Phrynosoma*, occur in western North America and Mexico and are characteristic of dry regions, where they feed primarily on ants.

Painted turtle *Chrysemys picta* (Emydidae) reaches about 51°N in North America. Freshwater and land turtles range southward to the limits of land in Africa and Australia (not Tasmania), and to northern Argentina in South America. One family, the Emydidae, is almost cosmopolitan in distribution, occurring on all continents except Australia and on many islands. The land turtles, Testudinidae, are also widespread except in Australia, but they are somewhat narrower in their latitudinal distribution than are the emydids. Among the reptiles, lizards hold the records in terms of latitudinal spread. In the north, the European wall lizard *Lacerta vivipara* (Lacertidae) reaches at least 70°N, the Slow worm *Anguis fragilis* (Anguidae) exceeds 64°N, and another lacertid, the Sand lizard *Lacerta agilis* exceeds 62°N. All of these lizards are European; no North American lizards exceed 51°N although this limit is reached by three species: the Short-horned lizard *Phrynosoma douglassi* (Iguanidae); the Western skink *Eumeces skiltonianus* (Scincidae); and the Northern alligator lizard *Gerrhonotus coeruleus* (Anguidae). Snakes also cross the Arctic Circle, in Europe at least where the Common viper *Vipera berus* (Viperidae) reaches about 67°N. The Common water snake *Natrix natrix* (Colubridae) reaches 65°N and other species exceed 60°N. Only one North American snake exceeds 60°N, the Common garter snake *Thamnophis sirtalis* (Colubridae) which reaches about 61°N. Other North American snakes range only as far north as about 52°N. In the south, lizards and snakes reach the limits of land in Africa, Australia and Tasmania and the lizards reach Tierra del Fuego at the southern tip of South America. Snakes do not range so far into South America where the southernmost species is a viper, *Bothrops ammodytoides*, which reaches southern Argentina. No terrestrial snakes are found on New Zealand, but two families of lizards reach this isolated southern outpost, the Scincidae and the Gekkonidae.

With the exception of salamanders, more species of amphibians and reptiles are tropical than are temperate or sub-polar in distribution. In fact, there is for amphibians and reptiles, as well as many other groups of animals and plants, a latitudinal gradient in number of species from poles toward the equator. This has been documented for the snakes of eastern Argentina. There are nine provinces or territories from Tierra de Fuego in the south to Misiones in the north, and the number of snake species in these is 0, 1, 5, 5, 15, 22, 32, 51, and 55. Similarly, we find five

The Thorny devil or Moloch of Australia, *Moloch horridus* is an ecological equivalent of the unrelated Horned lizard *Phrynosoma*.

species of amphibians and seven of reptiles in extreme southern Canada, with a relatively smooth increase in number of species as one moves southward to southern Texas where there are 20 species of amphibians and 73 of reptiles. There is no clear-cut explanation for the observed gradient although some, such as obvious climatic differences, seem intuitively to be obvious. The subject remains of considerable interest to ecologists.

Having roughly outlined the geographic ranges of the major groups of amphibians and reptiles, we must now ask how various families, genera and species have come to be distributed as they are. As we cannot discuss this in any great detail for a large number of groups, we will rely on a few examples, beginning at the family level, but a few words about Earth history are necessary first.

Continental Drift. Zoogeographic theory was once based entirely upon the rigid-Earth concept that the continents were immovable. If one wanted to explain the occurrence of an organism in, say, Africa and South America, it was necessary to postulate either that a land-bridge had once been such that movement between the hemispheres to the north was possible and that subsequent northerly extinction had resulted in isolation of populations on the two southern continents. This, of course, only applied to terrestrial organisms unable to cross a wide ocean barrier.

Southern biologists and geologists had long been uncomfortable with the concept of fixity of the continents, having noted the puzzle-like similarities of the eastern coastline of South America and the western coastline of Africa and the presence on the

The distribution of the glass snakes. They are limited to warm, subtropical regions. Note how only the largest island of the East Indies (Borneo) has been colonized.

119

southern continents of fossil floras and faunas of similar nature. It was suggested that possibly the continents of the south had once been united as a single large landmass, called Gondwanaland. As far back as 1912, Alfred Wegener, a German meteorologist, proposed the first comprehensive theory of continental drift, but without a known mechanism for moving the continents over the Earth's surface relative to one another, most biologists and geologists held firm to their conviction that the continents were forever firm in their positions. As recently as 1957, a noted zoogeographer could state quite convincingly that continental drift was a myth. This has all changed and there has resulted something of a revolution in the Earth sciences and, by extension, biogeography.

As more and more evidence accumulated that drift had occurred, geologists began more seriously to search for an explanatory mechanism. It was noted that the crust of the Earth, bearing the continents, was lighter than the material of the underlying mantle. The continents are, in a sense, floating on the mantle. Present theory has it that the surface of the Earth is composed of huge plates, all moving at the rate of from $\frac{1}{3}$–4 in (1–10 cm) a year relative to one another. The theory explaining the movements of the continents has come to be called plate tectonics. Simply explained, each plate is analogous to the top of a gigantic conveyer belt moving in one direction. It is driven by convection currents in the molten or semi-molten material within the mantle of the Earth. New material is added at the surface along rift zones where it is thrust up by volcanic activity. As the new material rises and cools, it is added to the trailing edge of the plate. One such clearly visible zone of upwelling constitutes the mid-Atlantic ridge. As one plate moves against another, its leading edge is forced downward. This often occurs at what are seen as deep oceanic trenches, and these are areas of frequent earthquakes. As surface material is returned into the mantle, it becomes molten or semi-molten again and is recirculated. There are several major plates (for example the African plate, the North American plate, and the Eurasian plate) and several minor plates (for example the Fiji plate and the Turkish plate), all moving relative to one another over the surface of the Earth. Therefore, the continents have not always been distributed over the face of the Earth as they are today, and continued movement dictates that they will not be so distributed in the future.

According to most reconstructions of past arrangements of the continents, all of them were united about 200 million years ago in a gigantic supercontinent called Pangaea. About 180 million years ago, the northern continents (North America and Eurasia) separated from the southern continents. The northern land mass is called Laurasia, the southern Gondwanaland. The Indian Subcontinent was part of Gondwanaland but soon broke away to move rapidly northward, colliding with the Eurasian land mass and pushing up the Himalayas in the process. This is still going on and the Himalayas continue to grow as a result. It is now easily explained why fossil marine organisms are found high in this mountainous region. By about 135 million years ago, South America and Africa had begun to separate, beginning in the south and initiating the formation of the South Atlantic Ocean. Crustal movements continued, with the continents moving to their present positions relative to one another and all except Antarctica moving in a generally northerly direction as well. As the continents moved northward, they moved through different climatic zones. Thus, the British Isles would have been near the equator in the Upper Permian and at 20°N in the Upper Triassic, rather than north of 50°N as they are today. The fauna of the British Isles would have been exposed to arid conditions in the Triassic.

This has been an oversimplified summary of the theory of continental drift, but it will serve as a basis for further discussion and the interested reader may find more detail in any of the many volumes devoted to drift that have appeared over the past few years. We can now consider the implications of continental drift to the distributions of families of amphibians and reptiles.

The Effects of Drift on Animals. The distributions of a number of amphibian and reptilian families suggest origins in either Laurasia or Gondwanaland. It has been suggested that there is a northern origin for the Cryptobranchidae, Salamandridae, Discoglossidae, Pelobatidae, Trionychidae, Dibamidae, Anguidae, Varanidae, Lanthanotidae, Typlopidae, Leptotyphlopidae, Aniliidae, Elapidae and Viperidae. A southern (Gondwana) origin is postulated for the caecilians, the Pipidae, Leptodactylidae, Bufonidae, Hylidae, Microhylidae, Iguanidae, Agamidae, Chamaeleontidae, Gekkonidae, Teiidae, Lacertidae, Cordylidae and Boidae. Richard Estes has recently reviewed the zoogeography of the clawed frogs (Pipidae). Today the pipid genus

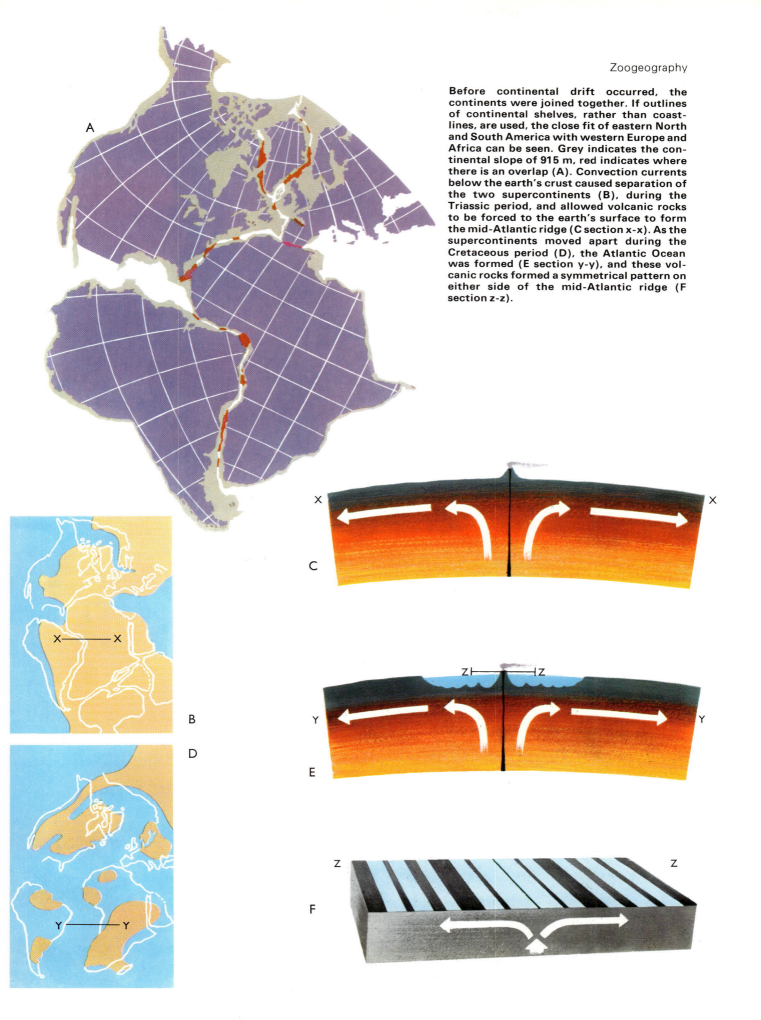

Before continental drift occurred, the continents were joined together. If outlines of continental shelves, rather than coastlines, are used, the close fit of eastern North and South America with western Europe and Africa can be seen. Grey indicates the continental slope of 915 m, red indicates where there is an overlap (A). Convection currents below the earth's crust caused separation of the two supercontinents (B), during the Triassic period, and allowed volcanic rocks to be forced to the earth's surface to form the mid-Atlantic ridge (C section x-x). As the supercontinents moved apart during the Cretaceous period (D), the Atlantic Ocean was formed (E section y-y), and these volcanic rocks formed a symmetrical pattern on either side of the mid-Atlantic ridge (F section z-z).

Xenopus is restricted to Africa and the family Pipidae occur naturally in Africa and South America where they are fully aquatic, freshwater frogs. The distribution of the family suggests an origin in Gondwanaland, specifically in the area made up of what are now parts of Africa and South America. As the continents drifted apart and the range of the family was split, different lines of pipid frogs evolved on the two continents from the common ancestors of Gondwanaland. Estes has discovered a fossil *Xenopus* from the Paleocene (about 60 million years ago) of Brazil and points out that forms intermediate to *Xenopus* and living South American pipids occur or occurred in both Africa and South America. Although living *Xenopus* can tolerate some salinity, it is doubtful that they or their ancestors could tolerate immersion in salt water long enough to have swum the Atlantic, even if it were once narrower. Also, there is no evidence that they were once distributed between Africa and South America through Europe and North America. Continental drift provided the barrier which divided the family, giving it its present distribution. At the family level, we have two examples of the effects of continental drift.

The lizard family Iguanidae is largely restricted to the western hemisphere, although genera also occur on Madagascar and the Fiji Islands. The family Agamidae is an eastern hemisphere representative and occurs in Africa, Australia, southeastern Europe and southern and southeastern Asia. The agamids and the iguanids are very similar to one another and most likely had a common ancestor in Gondwanaland. The two families diverged after the combined former range had been split by drift. A parallel situation is suggested for the lizard families Lacertidae (Old World) and Teiidae (New World). Both of these family-pairs are thought to have had common ancestors in the part of Gondwanaland which became Africa and South America. When continental drift is invoked to explain the distribution patterns of amphibians and reptiles, families or, rarely, genera are considered. The marine barriers caused by continental drift appeared so long ago to be useful in explaining the distributions of most genera and species and other events must be considered. Important among these were the glacial advances and retreats of the Pleistocene – the 'ice ages'.

Effects of the Ice Age. As we consider the Pleistocene, we are within a million years of today, and many of the present genera and some of the

living species had already made their appearance. In the northern hemisphere there were several glacial advances (glacials) during the Pleistocene separated by warmer periods (interglacials) during which the ice withdrew to the north. During the interglacials (we may be in the midst of one now), amphibian and reptile species expanded their ranges northward as climates there became more favourable. During the glacials, climatic zones were compressed southward, and species either shifted their ranges to remain within the same zone, or faced extinction. In addition, glacial ice tied up large amounts of the Earth's water and sea levels were lowered, exposing wide corridors along continental shelves along which animals could move to reach areas that later became islands. If several islands were on the same shallow bank, lower sea levels would have elevated the bank above sea level, making each of the areas which had been islands highlands on a single large island. With glacial retreat, sea levels once again rose, shutting off continental shelf corridors and isolating islands on their banks once again. All of these events affected the distribution of animals. We can see the effects of the Pleistocene in the distributions of two North American frogs. The Wood frog *Rana sylvatica* (Ranidae) ranges from Labrador to Alaska and to southern Canada in the west and to the southern Appalachian Mountains in the east. Isolated outlier populations are known from south of this range, in Idaho, on the Colorado–Wyoming border, in Kansas and Arkansas. The frog is adapted for the cool climates of boreal forests and we can explain the southern, isolated populations as relicts. That is, they were 'left behind'. The northern range of the Wood frog was covered with glacial ice during the Pleistocene, and the species' range shifted southward, covering the areas now inhabited by isolated populations. With the coming of an interglacial and retreat of the ice sheet, the range of the Wood frog shifted northward again, but populations of the frog remained behind in isolated areas of suitable habitat where local climatic conditions were favourable. This same pattern can be seen in the distribution of the Dakota toad *Bufo hemiophrys* (Bufonidae) which ranges through central Canada into north-central United States with a relict population in Wyoming near the location of the relict Wood frog population there. The Wyoming–Colorado population of *Rana sylvatica* has diverged sufficiently from the ancestral stock that it is no longer fully interfertile and it is now considered a distinct species, *Rana maslini*.

Again, in the United States, climatic shifts associated with advancing glaciation divided the ranges of several ancestral species of amphibians with the result that eastern and western subspecies of the Eastern spadefoot toad (*Scaphiopus holbrooki holbrooki* and *S. h. hurteri* respectively; Pelobatidae) evolved. The ranges of these two frogs do not presently overlap as the soils of the Mississippi embayment are not suitable and act as a barrier separating them. This same pattern is evidenced by the Ornate chorus frog *Pseudacris ornata* and Strecker's chorus frog *P. streckeri* (both Hylidae), but the area separating them is greater and, although morphologically quite similar, they are not interfertile and therefore have evolved to the species level.

Many of the species of amphibians and reptiles with distributions on the mainland and islands of the continental shelf owe their existence on the islands to Pleistocene changes in sea level. Such species became isolated on the islands when sea levels rose and some have diverged from the parental stock to the subspecies or species level. This is evident for many species of *Lacerta* (Lacertidae) on continental islands in the Mediterranean and Aegean Seas, for *Ameiva undulata miadis* (Teiidae) of Islas del Maiz in the Caribbean off Nicaragua, and for the anole *Anolis lemurinus* (Iguanidae) of the Bay Islands north of Honduras, to name but a very few. In desert regions, we sometimes find relict populations associated with water. Thus, the Arizona toad *Bufo microscaphus* (Bufonidae) has a spotty distribution in the arid southwestern United States in areas where suitable water is available. This probably represents a fragmentation of a more extensive range held during more mesic (moist) times in the Pleistocene. Wet-dry cycles (as opposed to warm-cool cycles) occurred even in the tropics during the Pleistocene, and these influenced the present distributional patterns and speciation (species formation) of animals. During dry periods, mesic 'islands' or refugia remained in which moist-adapted species could exist. If a species' range was divided with remnants in more than one refugium, speciation could occur and two species might occupy an area once occupied by one when moist conditions returned to the whole area. Conversely, in moist periods, arid refugia would operate. The history of the *Anolis chrysolepis* complex of the Amazon Basin has been attributed to this mechanism.

Of course, in order to inhabit any given area, a species must be adapted to the environmental conditions it faces there. We have alluded to this

repeatedly above. Thus, caecilians are restricted to tropical environments and do not tolerate low temperates. The Tailed frog *Ascaphus truei* (Leiopelmatidae) has been found to be active with body temperatures between about 39–57°F (4–14°C), whereas representatives of the essentially tropical family Leptodactylidae have been found to have body temperatures (when active) from about 72–84°F (22–28°C). In general, species or genera which exhibit broad temperature tolerances are more widely distributed than those with narrower tolerances. The same may be said with respect to tolerances for other environmental factors such as moisture. Of course, because of their tolerances with respect to one or more environmental factors, an area may act as a barrier to the spread of one species while serving as a corridor for the dispersal of another. For example, a subhumid corridor across northern Central America has been utilized by several species of amphibians and reptiles (for example *Hypopachus championi*, Microhylidae; *Cnemidophorus sacki motaguae*, Teiidae; *Leptodeira rhombifera*, Colubridae), but this same region, which extends through Guatemala and into Mexico, serves as a barrier to the dispersal of more moist-adapted species. Tolerances may be especially critical during the breeding season or as they affect young individuals. It has been suggested that summer temperatures are more important in explaining the northern distributions of amphibians than winter temperatures. Cold-adapted species may survive a long, cold winter and the population may prosper if summer temperatures are high enough for sufficiently long periods of time for reproduction to successfully occur. Although live-bearing reptiles are found at both high and low latitudes and elevations, they constitute a greater proportion of the reptilian fauna at high latitudes and elevations. Thus, five of the seven species of lizards and snakes which range above 60°N are live-bearers. Where a group of snakes has both egg-laying and live-bearing species in Asia and primarily live-bearers in North America, the Bering Strait land bridge, with its relatively cool climatic conditions, filtered out the egg-layers and allowed colonization of North America by live-bearing species. In cooler habitats such as are found at high latitudes and elevations, a non-moving egg clutch would be much more at the mercy of cold temperatures than a brood or clutch held internally by a mother that could move to more favourable conditions. Recent evidence suggests that the presence of a parietal eye

The Green tree snake *Dendrolaphis punctatus*, a species limited in its distribution to Western Australia.

has permitted some lizards to exploit higher latitudes (and possibly high elevations) through its partial control of thermoregulation and reproductive synchronization. Lizards without a parietal eye tend to be restricted to low latitudes, whereas those with functional parietal eyes occur at both low and high latitudes.

Colonization of Islands. Not all islands are on the continental shelf, and so we might ask the question 'how do amphibians and reptiles reach islands distant from a mainland or other island source area?' Furthermore, since not all amphibian and reptile species are equally good at colonizing oceanic islands, we should try to identify those characteristics which set successful colonists apart. We will omit from consideration sea-going species, such as sea turtles, sea snakes and some crocodilians (a crocodilian was the first large vertebrate to recolonize the island of Krakatoa following a spectacular volcanic explosion which killed all life in 1883), which simply arrive under their own power by swimming. For any terrestrial organism, arrival on an island far from the source area for a species is a chance event whose probability depends upon several factors. Two of the physical factors involved, for example, are the distance the island is from the mainland or another island, and how large the 'target'

island is. Other things being equal, it should be easier for a species to reach an island close to the source area than one more distant, and large islands should have a higher probability of being invaded than small islands if they are the same distance from the source. A distinction must be made here between invasion and colonization. The mere arrival of one or more individuals of a species on an island uninhabited by that species constitutes an invasion. The establishment of an on-going breeding population on the island is a colonization. Colonizations do not necessarily automatically follow from invasions. Many invasions are unsuccessful and even if colonization occurs, there is a certain probability of extinction. This probability is greater on small islands which may be more subject to environmental disasters (hurricanes, tidal waves) and on which the population may be restricted in size. For an invasion to be successful, that is, for a colonization to occur, the size of the pioneering group of individuals is important. For some species of animals, a single pregnant female may be sufficient to establish a population. For other species, which exhibit parental care for example, the minimum nucleus may be a pair. For social organisms, the number may be greater.

Organisms may reach islands in several ways aside from swimming or active flight. Small organisms may be carried by wind currents. This is the normal means of dispersal for certain spiders whose young spin out long web-strands which are caught by the wind and lift the spider off. The lifting winds of a hurricane might even transport an animal as large as a small frog, carrying it over considerable distances before setting it down unhurt. Of course, it would be extremely fortuitous if the frog were to land on an island, rather than in the much more extensive sea around it. Again, small organisms, such as algae and other microscopic animals and plants or plant seeds or spores might be carried from one place to another by larger animals. The mud on the feet of a migratory bird could harbour many individuals of such species, which would be liberated as the bird stopped or rested on an island. This means of dispersal is, however, unavailable to amphibians and reptiles so long as man is not considered the agent of dispersal. It seems that the most frequently employed mechanism by which larger terrestrial organisms reach islands is by rafting. A raft is any floating object large enough to support the organism in question. Rafts might be large enough to be considered floating islands, even carrying trees, which have broken off the banks of rivers emptying into the ocean. A few such large rafts have been sighted off North America, the Philippine Islands and the Moluccas, but they are undoubtedly uncommon. Most rafts are simply floating logs or mats of vegetation. In 1925 there was a report of an Eastern diamondback rattlesnake *Crotalus adamanteus* (Viperidae) on a water hyacinth raft off the coast of Florida, in 1929 there was a report of the arrival of a Boa constrictor *Boa constrictor* (Boidae) on St. Vincent Island in the Lesser Antilles, and a crocodilian which reached Barbados on the trunk of a tree. The latter two raftings probably originated from the Orinoco River of Venezuela. There is little doubt that, given the geological time scale available, rafting can explain the colonization of many oceanic islands even though the probability of any given raft carrying an organism which survives to land-fall and establishment of an insular population is slight. Remember that a low probability does not mean that something doesn't occur. It simply means that it doesn't occur very often and this is of relatively little importance when large time spans are available.

For a small amphibian or reptile, an extensive rafting experience presents certain difficulties and only some kinds have been successful as colonizers as a result. Freshwater might be expected to be in short supply on a raft and even rainwater would be 'salted' to some extent by spray. Thus, wholly aquatic freshwater amphibians make poor candidates for rafting, as do any organisms that require large quantities of fresh water. Certain kinds of food may be lacking or in short supply on rafts, so a good rafter must either be able to survive long periods without food or be able to make use of what is available. Smaller insectivorous lizards and frogs have seemingly been able to make these journeys by employing a combination of these two, whereas the few snakes which have arrived on islands most likely fasted for the duration of the trip unless they were able to exploit fellow travellers as a food source. Boids, which have proven themselves good colonizers, feed on mammals and birds for the most part, and would no doubt find such food restricted on a raft. Burrowing amphibians and reptiles are at a disadvantage in rafting and few have been able to colonize oceanic islands. The best colonists have been arboreal species, such as the anoles *Anolis* (Iguanidae), geckos *Hemidactylus* and *Thecadactylus* (Gekkonidae), tree frogs of the genera *Hyla* (Hylidae), *Eleutherodactylus* (Leptodactylidae), and *Rhacophorus* (Ranidae). There are, of course,

exceptions. Small terrestrial lizards like *Sphaerodactylus* (Gekkonidae) and various skinks (Scincidae) have been successful, as has the larger and more active lizard *Ameiva* (Teiidae). In general, however, amphibians and reptiles which have been successful at colonizing oceanic islands are small to moderate in size, relatively sedentary, arboreal and often nocturnal in habit.

Once a potential colonist or group of such individuals arrive on an island, there are other hurdles to be taken. If land-fall is on a beach, this must be crossed. For both amphibians and reptiles this involves exposure to predators. For diurnal organisms, the beach is essentially a desert devoid of freshwater and possibly very hot. For nocturnal amphibians, as well as diurnal species, the saltwater-soaked sand constitutes a formidable barrier that must be crossed quickly. If this barrier is successfully traversed, colonization can be the result only if a suitable habitat is found. This all implies that the tolerances of the organism must be in tune with the new environment it faces. Even if a suitable habitat is found, colonization may be prevented if it is already occupied by a species similar in habits and requirements to the new arrival. That is, if it is occupied by a species with an ecological niche similar to that of the invader. If this happens the invader may persist for a time but then be competitively excluded, becoming extinct on the island. Just such an occurrence has been reported on the island of Trinidad where *Anolis aeneus* is apparently competitively excluding *A. trinitatis*. Over a four year period, the ratio of *aeneus* to *trinitatus* shifted from 4:1 to 60:1 in one area, whereas *trinitatus* has been quite successful in areas unoccupied by *aeneus*. In this case, both species are native to the islands of the Lesser Antilles and have been introduced onto Trinidad. Extinction is not the only possible outcome of interaction between two similar species when they come together. Both may adjust in some way so as to divide the available resources between them. This has been documented for *Anolis* in the Caribbean. Size differences may evolve so that the two or more species on an island feed on prey items of different sizes and competition for food is thereby reduced. Or habitat shifts may occur such that the species do not overlap so much, one species being active primarily in the crowns of trees, another on the trunk, still another on low shrubs. Of course, the opposite can also occur. If a colonizing species comes from a source area where it was one of several similar species sharing the available resources, and if it finds itself on an island without such similar species, ecological release may occur. That is, the colonist may develop a broader ecological range (a wider ecological niche) than it had in the source area, occupying a wider range of habitats and exhibiting greater size variation and wider utilization of a broader spectrum of the available food items.

The various ideas we have introduced above apply for the most part to the colonization of new territory by continental species where barriers are salt water. As mentioned previously, a desert may be as much a barrier to a semi-aquatic amphibian as is salt water, and ponds or mesic areas surrounded by deserts can be viewed as ecological islands. Likewise, a stand of trees in a grassland is an island for the arboreal species inhabiting it, and an open area in a forest an island for those species restricted to such habitats. Therefore, the arid or mesic refugia in the Amazon Basin during the Pleistocene were ecological islands, as are the present southern enclaves occupied by the Dakota toad and the Wood frog in the United States.

We have said nothing about marine reptiles so far in our discussion. The distributions of these organisms are dictated in part by ocean currents and in part by the tolerances of the animals to temperature. In the Atlantic Ocean, for example, sea turtles are, as elsewhere, primarily tropical in distribution, but occasionally a Leatherback turtle or a Green turtle will be carried in the Gulf Stream northward where they have been sighted off New England in the United States. Currents have even carried sea turtles to the coast of the British Isles in this manner, although conditions there and in New England are not suitable for nesting and permanent populations have not been established. Temperature has played an important role in the distribution of sea snakes (Hydrophiidae) which occur in the Pacific and Indian Oceans, but not in the Atlantic. Temperatures encountered around the tips of South America and Africa have prevented sea snakes from entering the Atlantic. Also, they have not been able to cross the freshwater barrier of the Panama Canal.

Dispersal by Man. Man has become an important agent of dispersal for a wide variety of amphibians and reptiles, both deliberately and accidentally. Many secretive species have been transported from their native lands in cargo, and, at first, increasingly rapid means of transportation facilitated this. It was not unusual to find small Boa constrictors, tree frogs and lizards, as well as other arboreal amphibians

and reptiles (and invertebrates such as tarantulas!) in bunches of bananas shipped out of the tropics in the western hemisphere. These were usually single individuals and no colonizations were effected. With the advent of better packing methods and fumigation, this means of transport has largely disappeared. Burrowing amphibians and, especially, reptiles were and are occasionally transported in soil accompanying potted plants, but quarantine regulations have largely restricted this flow as well. It is the deliberate introductions that have most often resulted in successful colonizations by amphibians and reptiles.

The Marine toad *Bufo marinus* (Bufonidae) is a prime example. This tropical American species has been widely introduced on Pacific islands, including New Guinea, as an insect control measure. They have also been introduced into Florida in the United States. In many of the areas to which they have been introduced, Marine toads have multiplied to the extent that they are themselves serious pests. In the United States, there is the possibility that they will out-compete native species, especially as man modifies the environment and restricts the number of suitable breeding sites for the native species. Marine toads can tolerate high water temperatures as tadpoles, to 108°F (42°C), and develop rapidly. Like other toads, they have poison-secreting parotid glands but those of the Marine toad are especially large, as is the toad itself. The amount of venom secreted is sufficient to incapacitate or even kill a dog should one bite into the gland or swallow a toad.

As with the Marine toad, most deliberate introductions have an economic basis. At least 14 species of amphibians and reptiles have established breeding colonies in southeastern Florida following release by pet store owners or as accidents associated with commerce. Many other species are established in nonbreeding colonies in the same area. It is no longer possible to clearly delimit the natural ranges of certain economically important amphibians and reptiles because of their transport and release by man. This can come in the form of a turtle carried some distance by a small child before release, or the deliberate establishment of Bullfrogs *Rana catesbeiana* (Ranidae) as a food source, or various salamander species as a local supply of fish bait. During the Second World War, the Japanese introduced monitor lizards *Varanus* (Varanidae) onto a number of South Pacific islands as a source of food, and populations of these lizards are flourishing on some. These lizards occur naturally on many

Giant tortoises evolved on islands where they originally had no natural enemies. They are threatened with extinction on many islands, but survive on the Galapagos and Seychelles Islands. This is the Giant tortoise *Testudo elephantopus*.

nearshore islands in the Indonesian Archipelago, the Philippine Islands and off Australia. The entire amphibian and reptile fauna of Hawaii has resulted from human introductions, mostly accidental and from a wide variety of sources. Of course, man does not only promote establishment of amphibian and reptile populations but has been responsible for the decline of many species. We will have more to say about this in the next chapter.

The closing word in this chapter on zoogeography concerns not the distribution of species, but the occurrence of non-related ecological equivalents in similar habitats in different parts of the world. Thus we have the fringe-toed, sand-swimming lizards of the family Lacertidae, in Old World deserts which are similar in many respects to the fringe-toed lizard *Uma* (Iguanidae) of the deserts of the southwestern United States. Some of the African lacertids (for example *Nucrus*) occupy ecological niches similar to their counterparts among the Teiidae (*Ameiva* and *Cnemidophorus*) in the western hemisphere and the resemblances between species pairs are striking. One of the most spectacular

similarities involves the Moloch *Moloch horridus* (Agamidae) of Australia, and its ecological counterpart in North America, the Horned lizard *Phrynosoma* (Iguanidae). Both of these lizards are flattened and very spiny, both inhabit sandy deserts, and both depend very heavily on ants for food. To the uninitiated, the two lizards look like different species, but resemble one another closely enough that they might be placed in the same genus. Only an osteological study reveals their true relationships. A similar situation is revealed if one examines tree frogs of the family Hylidae and those of the genus *Rhacophorus* (Ranidae), or certain frogs of the genus *Rana* (Ranidae) and others of the genus *Leptodactylus* (Leptodactylidae). The ranges of hylids and *Rhacophorus* are nearly mutually exclusive, as are the New World ranges of *Rana* and *Leptodactylus*, and it is tempting to suggest that one does not invade the range of the other for competitive reasons. In all of these examples, the pairs show evidence of convergent evolution as a result of facing similar selective pressures and occupying similar ecological niches in different parts of the world.

127

Amphibians, Reptiles and Man

This chapter might have been titled 'Amphibians, Reptiles and Man: What They Do *For* Us, and What We Do *To* Them'. Unfortunately, the negative aspects of man's interactions with amphibians and, especially, reptiles have historically been emphasized in the popular press, and, in the interests of fair play, we will call attention to some of these. But amphibians and reptiles have contributed in significant ways to the benefit of mankind, and these contributions are too often overlooked. I believe that this is because they are more subtle and indirect than the benefits man derives from, for example, fishes and mammals, but they are important nonetheless. The foregoing chapters have been designed to introduce you to the wonderful diversity in life styles of amphibians and reptiles, and it is the intent of this closing chapter to increase your awareness of the significance of these under-rated animals to man.

The majority of reptiles and virtually all amphibians are harmless insofar as man is concerned. Snakes and crocodilians have received the most notoriety. Our concern here will be only with venomous species and not with the large constrictors (boas and pythons) so often depicted in the cinema as man-killers. There is only one record of one of these large snakes swallowing a person, that of a Reticulate python *Python reticulatus*, which attacked a 14 year old boy in the Talaud Islands of Malaysia. Most of these snakes are interested only in escape when confronted by a human and will attack only if provoked. This is true of virtually all snakes, but the consequences of a defensive bite from a venomous snake may be considerably greater than that of a non-venomous boid, large though the latter might be.

Venomous Snakes. Most of the dangerous venomous snakes belong to the families Viperidae,

The Eastern diamondback rattlesnake *Crotalus adamanteus* couples large adult size with large fangs and highly toxic venom, making it one of the most dangerous snakes in North America. This individual is defensively coiled, ready to strike.

Cobras are a favourite of snake charmers, including this one in West Pakistan. By swaying back and forth, the charmer causes the snake to do the same as it attempts to aim a strike. Some snake charmers employ a wind instrument also, but it is doubtful that the music has any effect on the snake. Some, but not all, snake charmers secretly remove the fangs of their snakes.

Elapidae, and Hydrophiidae. About 420 of the approximately 2,500 living species of snakes belong to these families, but many of these are either rare or secretive, or have venom which is not especially dangerous to man. There are also a few species of rear-fanged colubrids which are dangerous or potentially so to man. Most bites by venomous snakes are accidental. That is, the snake is encountered suddenly and unexpectedly and reacts quickly with a strike. For this reason, snake bite is a much more significant source of human mortality in parts of the world where shoes are not regularly worn and where shorts are worn instead of trousers. In Venezuela, for example, there are of the order of 3·10 deaths from snakebite per 100,000 individuals per year. For Ceylon, the figure is 4·20 and for India, 5·40. The total mortality from all causes in these countries is 990, 1,090 and 1,500, respectively. England and Wales, on the other hand, have a mortality rate resulting from the bites and stings of *all* venomous animals of only 0·02 with a total annual mortality of 1,140. It is apparent from these data that snakebite is not a major source of mortality even in those countries where it is most prevalent. There are probably more deaths annually as a result of bee and wasp stings than from snakebite. Most physicians rarely see a snakebite case and are not well trained in dealing with them.

There is also considerable disagreement among specialists as to the best treatment for snakebite with several different first aid techniques advocated. For these reasons, it is sometimes difficult to distinguish those patients who died from the bite from those who would have survived were it not for the treatment! Horse serum antivenin is often used to treat snakebite cases and individuals must be tested for sensitivity to horse serum before treatment is initiated. If not, a possibly fatal shock reaction can occur.

Snakebite can usually be avoided if simple precautions are taken. The first of these is to learn to recognize the venomous snakes in the area in which you live or travel. There are no universally useful means of recognizing venomous snakes of all kinds. Remember that some colubrids are rear-fanged and venomous. Although few are dangerous to man, the Boomslang *Dispholidus typus* of the savannas and scrub of south and central Africa has venom which is more toxic than those of the African viperids and elapids. In areas where venomous snakes are known to occur, always look before placing your feet or hands, especially in rocky areas or caves, and carry a light at night to illuminate the path in front of you. Never travel alone in areas where venomous snakes are abundant, and never deliberately aggravate one. Become familiar with one of the first aid treatments for snakebite and, if bitten, do not panic, apply first aid and get to a physician. Do not drink alcohol following a bite for this will speed the blood circulation and move the venom more rapidly from the site of the wound. Do not use morphine as a pain depressant because its effects combine with those of the venom to increase the potency of the venom. Of course, snakes are not the only venomous organisms

we should consider, but the venomous lizards (the Gila monster and Beaded lizard *Heloderma*, Helodermatidae) are rarely a source of worry – most bites come as an individual teases an animal, and the venoms of amphibians are more useful than dangerous to man and will be considered below.

Crocodiles. Large crocodilians are certainly at least potentially dangerous and there are many reports of attacks on man, many of which probably result from too close an approach to a nest. Although any large crocodile or alligator has the capability of severely injuring or killing a human, most species are rarely encountered and large individuals even less so. Only the Nile crocodile *Crocodylus niloticus*, and the Estuarine crocodile *C. porosus* (both Crocodylidae) have earned justified reputations as man-eaters. The Nile crocodile inhabits many river systems in tropical and southern Africa and Madagascar, whereas the saltwater crocodile ranges over a huge area from Ceylon and eastern India eastward to the Philippine and Fiji Islands, and southward through the Indonesian Archipelago to New Guinea and Australia. Both of these reptiles are aggressive and will stalk and attack people, probably in search of a meal. There are detailed and reliable reports of attacks by the Nile crocodile on small boats. P. B. M. Jackson describes a series of such encounters that took place along the shore of Mweru Wa Ntipa marsh near Lake Chisi in Zambia. As Jackson's boat progressed along the shore of the marsh, it was attacked by first one crocodile, then another, six to nine attacks in all. Jackson and others believe that crocodilians are irritated by the sounds of an outboard motor, and Jackson is of the opinion that the reptile's attacks are in defence of individual territories. Thus, an

The Mexican Beaded lizard *Heloderma horridum* (left) is one of the only two known venomous lizards; it rarely produces a fatal bite.

Crocodiles rarely attack man and, like many potentially dangerous animals, probably react only when they themselves are threatened. Only the Nile and Estuarine crocodiles, *Crocodylus niloticus* and *C. porosus*, have been known to initiate an attack on man.

attack by one crocodile was terminated as the boat left its territory only to be followed by an attack by another as the boat passed into a new territory. Such attacks are apparently more common in game preserves (Mweru Marsh is in a preserve) where the crocodilians have not had a history of harassment by man and attacks are infrequent outside these areas. It is worth noting that crocodilian attacks have been from the water. Other species of crocodilians, notably the Indian gavial *Gavialis gangeticus* (Gavialidae) and the Mugger crocodile *Crocodylus palustris* (Crocodylidae), have been found to contain human remains or artifacts such as bracelets and rings and thereby have been considered man-eaters. It is probable, however, that they are scavengers, eating corpses which fall from Indian funeral ghats. This is especially probable with respect to the gavial whose long, narrow, tooth-filled jaws are adaptations for fish eating.

Both amphibians and reptiles may serve as intermediate hosts or carriers of organisms which cause disease in man (pathogenic organisms). The importance of this from a public health standpoint has only been appreciated relatively recently and far too little information is yet available to assess it on a broad scale. Aquatic amphibians and reptiles are often implicated. Aquatic snakes and frogs are known to transmit both tapeworms and round-worms to humans if eaten. Freshwater turtles are notorious reservoirs for bacteria of the genus *Salmonella*. Salmonellosis results from an inflammation of the intestine and its symptoms include fever, diarrhea and vomiting. In the United States, baby turtles sold in pet stores were found to transmit the disease to humans and it is now illegal to sell turtles unless they have been tested and found free of *Salmonella*. Wild caught turtles, if found in the vicinity of human habitation, are suspect and care should be taken to wash the hands thoroughly after handling them. Turtles are not the only animals known to carry *Salmonella*. A recent survey of Panamanian amphibians and reptiles revealed infections of varying incidence in *Ameiva* and *Cnemidophorus* (Teiidae), *Sceloporus* and *Basiliscus* (Iguanidae), *Bufo marinus* (Bufonidae) and *Leptodactylus pentadactylus* (Leptodactylidae). The pathogens were most frequently isolated from specimens caught near houses, in pastures or at public bathing areas and none were found in representatives of 13

genera of frogs collected primarily in forested areas. Epidemics of salmonellosis are known to occur in a wide variety of domestic animals, such as turkeys, chickens and pigs, so the disease is of economic importance as well as from the standpoint of human health.

A few amphibians and reptiles have become pests, or are potentially pests, in areas where they have been introduced. We have already discussed one example, the Marine toad *Bufo marinus*, and another amphibian, the Clawed frog *Xenopus laevis* (Pipidae) has become established in and around San Diego in southern California where it has reached densities of pest proportions. These are fully aquatic frogs and are important as predators of small fish in the ponds in which they occur. Recently, one or more cobras have been found near homes in southern Florida and there is obvious concern that these highly venomous snakes will become established in the area.

The Edible frog *Rana esculenta* is important in both teaching and research, and is a source of food. The species inhabits Europe.

Uses to Man. Amphibians and reptiles are utilized as food in many parts of the world. Frogs' legs are considered a delicacy in the United States and Europe, and in Asia as well. This fact is reflected in the common name of *Rana esculenta* (Ranidae), the European edible frog. There has been some discussion of harvesting the large leptodactylid frogs of the Andean lakes of South America on a commercial basis. These are cooked whole. In Japan, the Giant asiatic salamander *Andrias japonicus* (Cryptobranchidae) is prized as a food item. Among the reptiles, turtles are often eaten and are considered a delicacy in oriental restaurants and households as well as elsewhere. Both the eggs and flesh of sea turtles, especially the Green sea turtle *Chelonia mydas* (Cheloniidae) are eaten. Lizards, especially the Green iguana *Iguana iguana* (Iguanidae) are

Lizards, especially larger species like this Common iguana *Iguana iguana*, are eaten by humans in many parts of the world. The meat of iguana is reputed to taste like chicken.

This is the common bullfrog of India, which serves as food both for humans and other animals as well as serving in teaching and research laboratories in southern Asia. The North American Bullfrog, a relative of both the European Edible frog and the Indian bullfrog, is similarly useful to man.

eaten locally, as are snakes. Rattlesnake steaks are sold as an exotic hors d'oeuvre in the United States. Attempts have been made to 'farm' both sea turtles and frogs as sources of food. Even crocodilians are eaten, especially the meat of the muscular tail.

Crocodilians are much more prized, however, for their skins, and over-exploitation has brought most species to the brink of extinction. The skins are turned into fine leather which is then made into shoes, handbags and other items. As the number of crocodilians, especially large individuals, has declined, the market value of hides has risen. Crocodilians are protected in many areas as a result of an increasing conservation-consciousness, but poaching still goes on and many species continue to decline. Protective measures have been successful where adequate enforcement has been provided, however, and the American alligator *Alligator mississipiensis* (Alligatoridae) has made a spectacular comeback in parts of its range in southeastern United States. In Louisiana and parts of Florida, it is now considered a pest and a limited hunting season or transplantation programme is under consideration. Hawksbill sea turtles *Eretmochelys imbricata* (Cheloniidae) were once in danger of extinction because the shell was valued commercially. Plastics have now largely replaced tortoiseshell, and so much of the commercial

pressure on these turtles has been removed, but they, along with the other sea turtles, are still considered endangered. The skins of various lizards and snakes have also been turned into leather for commercial sale, but the effects on the populations of the animals exploited has not been so dramatic as on the organisms cited above.

In some areas, a much more serious threat to amphibians and reptiles has come from professional collectors and the pet trade and, ironically, even from professional biologists who collect amphibians and reptiles for pets and museum collections. The Indigo snake *Drymarchon corais* (Colubridae) is valued as a pet because of its gentle nature, ease of maintenance in captivity and large adult size. It has been collected nearly to extinction over much of its range and is on several state endangered species lists in the United States. As amphibians and reptiles have gained popularity as pets, the import of exotic species has risen in some countries. In the United States, for example, Department of Interior statistics reveal that 582,407 live amphibians and 2,504,097 live reptiles were imported in 1972. The respective figures for 1967 were 137,697 and 405,134. Most of the amphibians and virtually all of the reptiles went directly into the pet trade, and probably the greater percentage of the animals were sold to individuals without the knowledge or facilities to adequately care for them. These animals, even if properly maintained, are rarely found to breed in captivity and so further imports are called for.

The venoms of both amphibians and reptiles have been employed for therapeutic purposes for centuries. Laboratories have been established for the production of antivenins and anavenins. Antivenins are produced by injecting sublethal doses of snake venom (or that of scorpions or other venomous organisms) into an animal, often a horse, so that the animal builds up an immunity to the venom. Serum is drawn from the animal and used to counteract the effects of a bite when it is injected into the victim. Anavenoms are simply slightly detoxified venoms which are used to build up an immunity to snake bite. Several so-called polyvalent antivenins are produced, each useful in the treatment of the bite of several species of snakes. Venoms are also used in other ways. The Indians of South America use the venom of frogs of the genus *Dendrobates* (Ranidae) to tip darts which are used in hunting. The venom is obtained by scraping the droplets off the skin of these small frogs as they are held over a fire and allowing the accumulated liquid to ferment. Darts are dipped in the substance and allowed to dry. Although the venom, in these doses, is not lethal to humans, it is to the small birds and mammals these Indians hunt. Death is by paralysis and slight exposure of the human tongue to the skin of one of these frogs leaves it numb. Toad venom has been employed by the Chinese both as a powder and in pill form for its supposed therapeutic value in the treatment of colds and inflammations. The venom does contain a number of substances which may be medically useful, such as cholesterol and epinephrine. There are many examples of amphibians or reptiles being used for medicinal purposes in the past. Some of these probably have no scientific basis, but others, such as the use of toad venom just cited, may have.

Finally, various species of amphibians and reptiles have found their places in teaching, research and clinical laboratories the world over. Most of the world's biologists and physicians gained their first introduction to the techniques of dissection and the wonders of anatomy with a frog. And comparative anatomists have employed a wide variety of amphibians and reptiles in their attempts to describe the functions of organs and organ systems in vertebrates. These studies have contributed immeasurably to our understanding of the evolution of

This Copperhead *Agkistrodon mokasen* is induced to eject its venom which is then used in the production of antivenin.

vertebrates. In the first chapter, we discussed the work of a biologist interested in the hormonal control of reproduction. This work is but another example of the use of these animals in research. In the clinical laboratory, the Clawed frog *Xenopus laevis* (Pipidae) was widely employed in pregnancy tests until better methods were devised. Other species of frogs have been used for the same purpose.

The overall importance of amphibians and reptiles in the biological control of pests has not been well documented as yet. Most farmers recognize the value of those snakes which feed on mice, and

The Greek or Hermann's tortoise *Testudo hermanni* has been exported from its native southern Europe as a pet to regions far north of its natural range.

tolerate them around their farm buildings. Lizards and toads may be locally effective in reducing the numbers of insects. For example, a single large American toad *Bufo americanus* (Bufonidae) ate 152 Mexican beetles in a day. At that rate, a single toad could eat 22,700 of these destructive beetles during the growing season from May till September. It would seem obvious that toads are valuable additions to the fauna in agricultural areas despite their warts and unappealing appearance.

The Indirect Effects of Human Activity. We have repeatedly mentioned the negative effects of human activities on populations of amphibians and reptiles. These might be viewed as direct assaults on these animals. We should also consider some of the destructive indirect effects of human activity, and it should be kept in mind that these indirect effects are felt not only by amphibians and reptiles but by other organisms such as fishes, birds and mammals as well. The most obvious indirect effect of human activity is habitat destruction. The clearing of land for buildings, the draining of swamps and marshes, the damming of rivers to form lakes, the heating of

water as a part of the cooling process of nuclear power plants, and the clearing of forests to claim agricultural land all reduce the amount of suitable habitat not only for one or two species of organisms but for the entire natural communities of which they are part. Some species have very small ranges and very little disturbance could result in total extinction. Extreme examples are afforded by the Valdina Farms salamander *Eurycea troglodytes*, the San Marcos salamander *Eurycea nana* and the Honey creek cave blind salamander *Eurycea tridentifera*. These lungless salamanders (Plethodontidae) are each restricted to a single spring or cave site in Texas and are, therefore, totally dependent upon the good will of man for their survival.

Of course, some species of amphibians and reptiles prosper in the company of man. Whereas stream-dwelling amphibians might be exterminated in the lake formed by a dam, lake-dwelling species thrive and find new habitats. Conversion of land to rice paddies and irrigation of arid lands provides previously unavailable habitats for aquatic or moisture-loving species. Walls and hedges around

The Clawed frog *Xenopus laevis* of Africa found wide use in the clinical laboratory for pregnancy tests, but has become a pest outside its natural range, as in southern California, where it has been introduced by man.

fields and buildings provide retreats for other species. A ready supply of insects and rodents around human habitation attracts still others. It has been suggested that populations of the lizard *Ameiva ameiva* (Teiidae) in Panama owe their existence to the agricultural corridor that existed between Panama and northern South America during the time of Columbus. These savanna-dwelling lizards do not inhabit the forests that now close the gap between the grasslands of central Panama and South American savannas. Animals, including *Ameiva*, which prefer open habitats are expanding their ranges along paths and roads as the rainforests of the Amazon basin are cleared to make way for civilization. Such animals prosper as others become extinct.

Both amphibians and reptiles have been affected by the addition of DDT and other insecticides to their environments. Significant mortality has been reported among these animals following the use of a chemical called heptachlor in large areas of the United States in an attempt to control fire ants. DDT and its breakdown products are not metabolized by animal systems and accumulate in body tissues. When they reach certain levels, they affect the central nervous system and death results. Whereas a single small frog may contain only a small, subtoxic level of such an insecticide, a snake may eat many frogs and retains the total pesticide dose carried by all. The snake may then be eaten by a hawk, which has also eaten other snakes or prey items carrying loads of pesticide, and eventually this so-called top carnivore accumulates a toxic load. Even subtoxic loads may be important, for it is widely recognized that birds carrying even these levels of DDT produce eggs with such thin shells that they often break prior to full development of the embryo.

There is now an increasing awareness that individual species are components of natural communities, and that the welfare of each species contributes to the welfare of the whole community. Each endangered species should be viewed as a symbolic alarm with respect to the entire ecosystem of which it is a part. As more and more species in an ecosystem become endangered, louder grows the alarm. This should be linked to the realization that human health and welfare are directly linked to environmental health and welfare. A certain level of modification of, and interference in, the functioning of natural communities and ecosystems is and will be necessary to carry out the goals of mankind. But man himself is but one species, one component in the world community. As the dominant member of that community, man exerts life and death control over other elements of the community but his own activities and welfare are inextricably linked to the whole. In the long run, how man treats his environment will affect his own welfare. Some attempts are being made to preserve components of natural communities and ecosystems, including amphibians and reptiles. A number of species have been granted legal protection through various endangered species acts. Thus, the Tuatara is now strictly protected in New Zealand and the Gila monster in the state of Arizona in the United States. Crocodilians are totally protected, or partially so through controlled hunting, in several parts of the world, and the state and city of New York has legislated against the sale of crocodilian hides, an important move inasmuch as New York is one of the capitals of the fashion world. Unfortunately, other fashion centres have not followed suit and hides remain valuable enough to encourage poaching. Sea turtles of all species are also protected in many countries where they nest, but here again poaching is a problem. Even many of the less notable species have been afforded local protection. Australia strictly controls the export of all of its wildlife, and 38 member countries of the African Convention of Conservation of Nature and Natural Resources has provided total legal protection to several endangered amphibian and reptilian species. Many of the states of America have laws governing species judged endangered within their borders, but enforcement of these is lax in many of these states.

Unfortunately, much of the recent flurry of activity to protect rare and endangered species may be too late for some. Minimum viable population levels may already have been achieved or surpassed. We have so little ecological information on most species of amphibians and reptiles that it is usually impossible to say how large a preserve should be set aside to protect a given species, and the problems are compounded as one realizes that, in order to preserve the species, we must preserve its environment and the natural community of which it is a part. Some extinctions resulting from man's activities are, therefore, inevitable at this date, but others may be prevented. It is to man's long-term advantage to do so. Not only would he be preserving some sparkling examples of the diversity of nature, but he would be contributing to the maintenance of ecological balance so necessary for his own survival.

Classification of Amphibians and Reptiles

Class Amphibia

*SUBCLASS LABYRINTHODONTIA
*ORDER Ichthyostegalia
*ORDER Temnospondylia
  *SUBORDER Rhachitomi
  *SUBORDER Stereospondyli
  *SUBORDER Plagiosauria
*ORDER Anthracosauria
  *SUBORDER Schizomeri
  *SUBORDER Diplomeri
  *SUBORDER Embolomeri
  *SUBORDER Seymouriamorpha

*SUBCLASS LEPOSPONDYLI
*ORDER Nectridea
*ORDER Aistopoda
*ORDER Microsauria

SUBCLASS LISSAMPHIBIA
SUPERORDER SALIENTIA
*ORDER Proanura (Ancient Frogs)
 ORDER Anura (Frogs)
  SUBORDER Archaeobatrachia
   FAMILY Leiopelmatidae
   FAMILY Discoglossidae (Fire-bellied and Midwife Toads)
   FAMILY Rhinophrynidae (Burrowing Toads)
   FAMILY Pipidae (Tongueless Frogs)
   FAMILY Pelobatidae (Spadefoot Toads)
  SUBORDER Neobatrachia
   FAMILY Myobatrachidae
   FAMILY Rhinodermatidae (Mouth-breeding Frogs)
   FAMILY Leptodactylidae
   FAMILY Bufonidae (True Toads)
   FAMILY Brachycephalidae
   FAMILY Dendrobatidae (Poison-dart Frogs)
   FAMILY Pseudidae
   FAMILY Centrolenidae (Glass Frogs)
   FAMILY Hylidae (True Tree Frogs)
   FAMILY Ranidae (True Frogs)
   FAMILY Sooglossidae
   FAMILY Microhylidae
SUPERORDER CAUDATA
 ORDER Urodela (Salamanders)
  SUBORDER Cryptobranchoidea
   FAMILY Hynobiidae (Asiatic Salamanders)
   FAMILY Cryptobranchidae (Giant Salamanders and Hellbenders)
  SUBORDER Sirenoidea
   FAMILY Sirenidae (Sirens)
  SUBORDER Salamandroidea
   FAMILY Proteidae (Olms)
   FAMILY Necturidae (Mud Puppies)
   FAMILY Amphiumidae (Congo Eels)
   FAMILY Salamandridae (Salamanders and Newts)
  SUBORDER Ambystomatoidea
   FAMILY Ambystomatidae
   FAMILY Plethodontidae (Lungless Salamanders)
SUPERORDER GYMNOPHIONA (Caecilians)
 ORDER APODA
   FAMILY Ichthyophidae
   FAMILY Typhlonectidae
   FAMILY Scolecomorphidae
   FAMILY Caeciliidae

Class Reptilia

SUBCLASS ANAPSIDA
*ORDER Cotylosauria (Cotylosaurs)
*ORDER Mesosauria (Mesosaurs)
 ORDER Chelonia or Testudines (Turtles)
  *SUBORDER Proganochelydia
  *SUBORDER Amphichelydia
  SUBORDER Cryptodira
   FAMILY Dermatemydidae (Central American River Turtle)
   FAMILY Chelydridae (Snapping Turtles)
   FAMILY Kinosternidae (Musk and Musk Turtles)
   FAMILY Testudinidae (Land Tortoises)
   FAMILY Platysternidae (Big-headed Turtle)
   FAMILY Emydidae
   FAMILY Cheloniidae (Sea Turtles)
   FAMILY Dermochelyidae (Leatherback Sea Turtle)
   FAMILY Carettochelyidae (New Guinea Plateless Turtle)
   FAMILY Trionychidae (Soft-shell Turtles)
  SUBORDER Pleurodira (Side-neck Turtles)
   FAMILY Pelomedusidae (True Side-neck Turtles)
   FAMILY Chelyidae (Snake-necked Turtles)

SUBCLASS LEPIDOSAURIA
*ORDER Eosuchia (Eosuchians)
 ORDER Rhynchocephalia (Beaked Reptiles)
   FAMILY Sphenodontidae (Tuatara)
 ORDER Squamata (Scaly Reptiles; Squamates)
  SUBORDER Sauria (Lizards)
   FAMILY Gekkonidae (Geckos)
   FAMILY Pygopodidae (Flap-footed Lizards)

FAMILY Dibamidae
FAMILY Anelytropsidae
FAMILY Iguanidae
FAMILY Agamidae
FAMILY Chamaeleontidae (True or Old World
   Chamaeleons)
FAMILY Scincidae (Skinks)
FAMILY Cordylidae (Girdle-tailed Lizards)
FAMILY Lacertidae
FAMILY Teiidae
FAMILY Anguidae
FAMILY Anniellidae (California Legless Lizards)
FAMILY Xenosauridae
FAMILY Helodermatidae (Gila Monster and Beaded
   Lizard)
FAMILY Varanidae (Monitor Lizards)
FAMILY Lanthanotidae (Earless Monitor Lizard)
FAMILY Xantusiidae (Night Lizards)
SUBORDER Amphisbaenia (Amphisbaenians)
  FAMILY Amphisbaenidae (Side-toothed
    Amphisbaenians)
  FAMILY Bipedidae (Two-legged Amphisbaenians)
  FAMILY Trogonophidae (Tip-toothed
    Amphisbaenians)
SUBORDER Serpentes (Snakes)
  FAMILY Typhlopidae (Blind Snakes; Worm Snakes)
  FAMILY Leptotyphlopidae (Slender Blind Snakes)
  FAMILY Aniliidae
  FAMILY Xenopeltidae (Sunbeam Snakes)
  FAMILY Uropeltidae (Shieldtail Snakes)
  FAMILY Boidae (Boas and Pythons)
  FAMILY Acrochordidae (Wart Snakes)
  FAMILY Colubridae
  FAMILY Viperidae (Old World Vipers and Pit Vipers)
  FAMILY Elapidae (Cobras, Coral Snakes and their
    relatives)
  FAMILY Hydrophiidae (Sea Snakes)

SUBCLASS ARCHOSAURIA (Ruling Reptiles)
*ORDER Thecodontia
 ORDER Crocodylia (Crocodilians)
    FAMILY Alligatoridae (Alligators)
    FAMILY Crocodylidae (True Crocodiles)
    FAMILY Gavialidae (Gavial)
*ORDER Saurischia (Dinosaurs)
*ORDER Ornithischia (Dinosaurs)
*ORDER Pterosauria (Pterosaurs; Flying Reptiles)

*SUBCLASS EURYAPSIDA
*ORDER Araeoscelidia
*ORDER Sauropterygia
*ORDER Placodontia
*ORDER Ichthyosauria

*SUBCLASS SYNAPSIDA (Mammal-like Reptiles)
*ORDER Pelycosauria
*ORDER Therapsida

---

* indicates an extinct group. Extinct families are not listed.

Index

Italics are used for generic and specific names and also to indicate pages on which illustrations appear.